THE REAL ESTATE INVESTMENT ADVISOR

The '90s Guide to Buying and Selling Real Estate

G. Timothy Haight & Daniel D. Singer

PROBUS PUBLISHING COMPANY
Chicago, Illinois

This publication is designed to provide accurate and authoritative information in regard to the subject matter covered. It is sold with the understanding that the publisher is not engaged in rendering legal, accounting or other professional service. If legal advice or other expert assistance is required, the services of a competent professional person should be sought.

Library of Congress Cataloging in Publication Data Available

ISBN 1-55738-186-0

Printed in the United States of America

BC

2 3 4 5 6 7 8 9 0

Dedication

Dedicated with love to my mother, Virginia Catherine, and father, Chester Dale Haight.

Tim Haight

Dedicated with love to my mother, Winifred, and father, Daniel Singer.

Dan Singer

Contents

Preface

This book is designed to help you identify personally profitable real estate opportunities in the depressed real estate market of 1991. Real estate market conditions are currently in a state of flux. The recession of 1990, overbuilding in a number of real estate markets during the last half of the 1980s, the savings and loan crisis, and the difficulties of commercial banks have all contributed to an aura of chaos in the market. Real estate markets that have only gone up for 20 or 30 years are suddenly flat, or worse, falling.

The present situation will not last indefinitely. We feel that the present situation is only temporary and now is the time for investors of courage and wisdom to make appropriate investments in real estate. This book will not make you rich overnight. However, *The Real Estate Investment Advisor* will help you systematically identify and evaluate alternative real estate projects.

This book will provide the reader with an understanding of the underlying factors which spell the success or failure of various real estate investments. By providing the tools necessary to understand real estate investing, the reader is able to screen possible investment opportunities and identify those factors which are critical to the success of the project. Furthermore, this book will enable the investor to properly evaluate real estate investment opportunities based on their underlying economic merits.

The book is divided into four parts. The first part provides the reader with the background necessary to evaluate real estate as an investment. This section details the various forms of real estate ownership, highlighting the strengths and weaknesses of each. In addition, traditional financial tools such as financial statement analysis, breakeven analysis, and present value analysis are illustrated in great detail. The impact of financial leverage, and tax reform, are also examined in-depth.

The second part provides the reader with an overview of the traditional types of real estate investments. The topics discussed include individual home ownership, apartment complexes, condominiums, and historic rehabilitation projects. Each chapter details the unique characteristics of that type of real estate investment, its strengths and weaknesses, and provides an illustration of a hypothetical investment.

The third part presents the reader with an overview of several aggressive types of real estate investments. The topics discussed include office buildings, industrial projects, land development, shopping centers, low income housing, mini-storage parks, and mobile home parks. Each chapter details the unique characteristics of that type of real estate investment, its strengths and weaknesses, an provides an illustration of a hypothetical investment which will enable the reader to grasp the critical factors in making a given investment a success.

The fourth part of this book presents a model software system for evaluating real estate limited partnerships. Most of the analysis in *The Real Estate Investment Advisor* assumes individual ownership. Many of the types of projects contemplated as real estate investments are suitable for limited patnerships—indeed, limited partnerships are often the most suitable vehicles for ownership. This chapter will help the investor understand the complexities of these sophisticated financial vehicles.

Individuals desiring to purchase the Real Estate Limited Parntership Analyzer should send a check for $99 to Probus Publishing Company, 1925 N. Clybourn Avenue, Chicago, IL 60614.

We hope that this book will be helpful to all those investors, both large and small, who are considering investing in real estate.

Acknowledgements

This book was written with the help of many individuals who have given invaluable assistance. First of all we are indebted to our families and loved ones who have sacrificed so much in allowing us to spend the time necessary to research and write this book. Without their understanding, this work could not be accomplished.

We would also like to express our gratitude to Probus Publishing Company, a constant source of encouragement throughout this project.

We wish to thank the University community at Towson State for their generous support and encouragement. In particular, we wish to acknowledge President Hoke Smith, Provost Robert Caret, and Dean Sam Barone for their support of our efforts.

A note of special thanks to several members of the Baltimore business community who have aided us in our research efforts. In particular, Jay Atkinson (Baker Watts), Robby Boyd (Mercantile-Safe Deposit and Trust Company), W. Talbot Daley (Legg Mason), Robert Frank, (Alex. Brown & Sons), Ronald R. Frederick (Saab Aircraft of America, Inc.), Matt Glenn (Legg Mason), Douglas Hicks (Hichs & Rotner), James Plitt (Clifton Trust Bank), Judy Plowman (Coldwell Banker), Gary Potts (Pizza Hut), Andrew Long III (Attorney), Georges F. Rocourt (Mercantile-Safe Deposit and Trust Company), Glenn E. Ross (Mercantile-Safe Deposit and Trust Company), Steve Jones (Gempler Realty), Richard Clarke (Marcor), and Alvin Schugam for their assistance.

G. Timothy Haight
Daniel D. Singer

Chapter 1

An Introduction to Real Estate Investing

The fishing is often the best in a storm. So too, in real estate. The real estate market is troubled in 1991. Demand has been softened by the recession of 1990. Much of the Southwest still has not recovered from the aftermath of falling petroleum prices. Many metropolitan areas were overbuilt in the 1980s. Speculative excesses by commercial banks and savings and loans resulted in a downward spiral of prices in some real estate sectors as these financial institutions attempted to liquidate their real estate assets under near-panic conditions. The regulatory reaction to these excesses has resulted in a tightening of credit standards which further reduced the effective demand for real estate.

All of this has led to an abundance of great investment opportunities. The real estate market will recover. The population will grow and demand more housing. Business will expand and need factories and office buildings. Today's problem is not finding a good real estate investment, it is selecting from the many opportunities confronting the individual investor. *The Real Estate Investment Advisor* is designed to help you do exactly that.

There are many ways to evaluate the return on an investment. This book uses the concept of discounted net cash flow relative to investment outlay for evaluating specific investments and comparing alternative investments. This may be expressed in terms of absolute dollars as in net present value or as a percentage in the internal rate of return. This approach has the advantage of permitting investors to maximize the true return on their investments. It incorporates all forms of returns, cash and noncash expenses, timing variations, and taxes at all levels and facilitates the comparison of markedly different types of investment opportunities.

This chapter presents a brief overview of the many forms of real estate ownership available today, as well as the advantages and disadvantages associated with real estate investing in general. Knowing what investment choices are available and recognizing the risks and benefits involved with each is an important first step in successful real estate investing.

3

Table 1.1 Advantages and Disadvantages of Ownership Forms

Form	Control	Personal Liability	Liquidity	Taxes
Direct:				
Individual Ownership	Full	Full	Determined by local market conditions. Lack of diversification suggests high risk.	Profits subject to personal income tax. Losses may offset earned income to give a maximum tax savings of $8,333.
Indirect				
General Partnership	Full	Full for general partners	Lack of liquidity.	Profits and losses treated as those for individually owned property. Losses do not have to be distributed proportionately.
Limited Partnership	None for limited partners	Limited to investment for limited partners	Some limited partnership shares are highly liquid and actively traded on major stock exchanges.	Same as General Partnership, unless units are actively traded.
Real Estate Investment Trusts (REITs)	Control by managers	Limited to investment	Many REITs are highly liquid and actively traded on major stock exchanges.	Profits flow through to individuals without double taxation. Losses can not be passed on to investors.
S Corporation	Control by managers	Limited to investment	Small market for equity interest suggest lack of liquidity.	Profits and losses treated on a pro rata basis for individually owned property as above.
Corporation	Control by managers	Limited to investment	Highly liquid for stocks listed on the major exchanges.	Profits received in the form of dividends subject to taxation at both the corporate and individual level.

The advantages and disadvantages of alternative ownership forms are summarized in Table 1.1. Which form of real estate investment is best depends on the investors' need for control and their willingness to accept greater risk for higher return.

Benefits of Real Estate Investing

Tax Advantages

Real estate has traditionally been a high-yielding investment, often generating net returns higher than those obtained by fixed-income securities. Tax benefits play a critical role in providing real estate investors with these high after-tax returns. Investors are allotted depreciation deductions as well as sizable tax credits in some instances, and these benefits enable real estate holders to receive substantial tax-free cash flows.

Amendments in 1990 to the Tax Reform Act of 1986 effectively raised marginal tax rates. Real estate can still offer a shelter from high taxes. While it is impossible to predict future tax changes, it is likely that taxes will go higher and that tax shelters (such as real estate) will become more important.

Leverage

Typically, when real estate is purchased only part of its cost is composed of owner's capital. The remainder of the required funds are secured by a mortgage on the property. In fact, 80 percent or more of real estate acquisition costs are often financed with debt. The use of leverage not only allows investors to control investments many times greater than their cash investment, but it can also magnify the return that investors experience on their invested capital as well. Thus, the ability to "lever" real estate may provide investors with greater returns than those available if investors use only their own capital.

Inflation Hedge

In addition, real estate has frequently proven an effective hedge against inflation. The increasing cost of new construction tends to drive up property values. Economic growth in an area with a fixed stock of improved real estate causes property values to soar. Rental income, for example, can be periodically adjusted to keep pace with inflation. Tenants may be required to share in operating cost increases under the terms of their lease agreements. This ability to outpace inflation suggests that real estate should be a part of many investor's portfolios.

Risks of Real Estate Investing

As in most other types of investment opportunities available today, there are risks involved in real estate investing. First of all, the transaction costs associated with buying and selling real estate can be substantial. Selling commissions often run seven percent or more of real estate's selling price. The cost of these commissions combined with state and local transfer taxes, documentary stamps, and other fees associated with real estate transactions may necessitate a longer holding period than that required for investing in financial assets.

Lack of liquidity is another disadvantage of real estate investments. Liquidity is the ability to quickly turn property into cash without loss of value. The illiquidity of real estate investments is caused at least partly by the typically large transaction size, which creates a market open to a relatively small number of potential buyers. As shown in the next section, some ownership forms minimize the lack of liquidity problems inherent in real estate investing.

Unlike financial assets that can be held by a broker, real estate must be managed. Rental property may require leasing and the active management of tenants. Other administrative expenses and accounting activities require an expenditure of time and money on the part of the owner.

Price volatility may also characterize real estate investments. The use of leverage in real estate investing makes property values highly sensitive to interest-rate fluctuations. Since the stock of property does not change rapidly, when economic conditions change quickly and substantially, property values also change substantially. Abrupt changes in the income tax code, property tax rates, and zoning laws can have a dramatic effect on the price of real estate.

Additionally, gauging the true value of real estate is difficult at best. Whereas market values of financial assets such as stocks and bonds are readily available, real estate comparables are more difficult to obtain. Location, physical characteristics, and revenue and expense characteristics, as well as lack of transaction volume make comparisons imprecise. Therefore, it is much more difficult to gauge the "true" value of real estate.

Forms of Real Estate Ownership

The form of ownership has a direct influence on the investors' return and risk. Investors can own real estate either individually or collectively. Furthermore, ownership can be held directly (i.e., name on the deed) or indirectly (i.e., through the ownership of real estate securities). Each of these forms has advantages and disadvantages.

Direct Ownership

The forms of direct real estate ownership include sole ownership, tenants in common, joint tenancy, and tenants in the entirety. Each of these has specific advantages and disadvantages that investors must consider when selecting the form in which they want to hold real estate.

Sole Ownership. Sole ownership is the most flexible form of real estate ownership, since the property is possessed by one individual. Under this form, the owner receives all of the benefits from real estate ownership. All income and/or tax benefits flow directly to the sole owner, and that person is free to dispose of the property as he or she sees fit, subject to legal constraints. Under this form of ownership, the individual's liability is unlimited.

Tenants in Common. The tenants in common form of ownership exists in instances where two or more individuals own an individual real estate property. Under this form of ownership, each participant owns an "undivided interest" in a property, the property or its rights cannot be controlled or disposed by any individual participant. Each participant has a stated interest in the whole property (these interests do not have to be equal) and her or his liability is based on a proportionate share of ownership. Each participant is free to sell or otherwise transfer her or his interest in the property without the consent of the other owners. Tenants in common are treated as individuals rather than as a corporation for tax purposes. There is no right of survivorship under the tenants in common form of ownership.

Joint Tenancy. Unlike the tenants in common arrangement, the joint tenancy form of ownership requires equal ownership of property, with each owner entitled to the right of survivorship. In the event of the death of one or more of the owners, her or his interest is passed on to the survivor(s). The joint tenancy form of ownership requires that four unities exist: title, time, interest, and possession. In the event that one or more of these unities does not exist, then the ownership form is tenants in common.

Tenants in the Entirety. A type of joint tenancy, tenants in the entirety exists when a husband and wife own a piece of property. Under this form of ownership, the property cannot be transferred without the signatures of both the husband and wife. In the event of the death of one spouse, the surviving spouse gains full ownership of the property.

Indirect Ownership

The forms of indirect real estate ownership include general partnership, limited partnership, real estate investment trust, and corporation. Each of these forms gives investors a degree of liquidity and has advantages and disadvantages.

General Partnership. General partnership is an association of two or more individuals formed for the purpose of making a profit. Each partner has unlimited liability. The transfer of real estate ownership requires the permission of all partners. The general partnership serves as a conduit in which income is taxed at the individual level. Each partner is fully liable for all claims against the general partnership.

Limited Partnership. The limited partnership provides an exceptionally attractive way of owning real estate for many investors. Traditional limited partnerships may be created to acquire real estate for investment purposes. These partnerships are actually comprised of two types of partners: general and limited. General partners are responsible for carrying out the day-to-day responsibilities of the business. In return for a fee, the general partners provide professional expertise, actively managing the partnership's assets and making all of the business decisions. In addition, the general partners assume unlimited liability on behalf of the partnership.

The limited partners provide most of the capital required to fund the operations of the partnership. They are not permitted to engage in the business activities of the partnership, and their liability is usually limited to the amount that they contribute and/or pledge.

The limited partnership itself is generally not a taxable entity; it serves as a conduit in which profits and losses flow through to the individual level. These profits and losses can be allocated to each partner differently as long as there is a sound business purpose for doing so. In return for their equity contribution, the partnership allocates most of the profits and cash distributions to the limited partners, based on a sharing arrangement stipulated in the partnership agreement.

Tax regulation determines whether an organization will be treated as a limited partnership (with profits and cash flowing through directly to the partners) or as a corporation (with profits taxed at both the organization and individual level).

A major disadvantage of limited partnerships is that the limited partners are generally locked into their investment until such time as the general partners wish to dissolve the partnership. However, one type of limited partnership reduces this lack of liquidity.

Master Limited Partnership. Master limited partnerships (MLP) provide investors with liquidity, since they are actively traded on the New York and American stock exchanges, as well as in the over-the-counter market. However, as a result of passage of the 1987 Budget-Reconciliation Act, income from master limited partnerships as well as "readily tradable" partnerships cannot be used to offset losses generated from passive investments. Furthermore, MLPs created after December 17, 1987 are to be treated as corporations for tax purposes; MLPs created before that date are exempt from this law until 1998 if certain investment conditions are met.

There are three types of master limited partnerships: roll-up, roll-in, and roll-out. A roll-up MLP raises capital through the issuance of securities (master limited partnership units) and uses these funds to acquire interests of several smaller limited partnerships. A roll-in MLP uses proceeds from primary offerings to purchase real estate property directly. A roll-out MLP is created when a corporation creates a master limited partnership and then sells its real estate holdings to that MLP.

Real Estate Investment Trust. Real estate investment trusts (REITs) have become increasingly popular with investors. Their popularity can be easily understood, as these trusts provide many financial opportunities and tax benefits that would normally not be available to individual investors. As high-yielding investments, REITs have enjoyed unparalleled success.

Real estate investment trusts have experienced rapid growth since Congress passed the Real Estate Investment Trust Act of 1961. REITs provide individual investors with the opportunities to participate in larger real estate investments. These trusts can acquire real estate directly (equity REITs), indirectly (mortgage REITs), or by a combination of the two (hybrid REITs). REITs have many advantages as investments: federal tax-exempt status, use of professional managers, ease of achieving liquidity, ability to leverage investments, and provision of diversification to the individual investor.

To qualify for favorable tax treatment a REIT must distribute at least 95 percent of its earnings to shareholders, hold at least 75 percent of its assets in the form of real estate, generate at least 75 percent of its earnings from real estate activities, and have at least 100 shareholders. If these and other requirements are not met, the entity can lose its tax exempt status.

Corporation. The corporate form of ownership offers many advantages. It allows access to capital markets for fund-raising through the issuance of stock. Once sold to the public, the stock can be transferred freely without affecting the operations of the corporation. In addition, the owners' liability is limited to the amount of capital invested. For tax purposes the corporation is treated as an entity in and of itself. Profits are taxed at corporate rates. Dividends paid out of after-tax profits are again taxed at the individual level.

S-Corporation. A special type of corporation, the S-corporation, enjoys the benefits of the corporate as well as individual ownership form. For the most part S-corporations are treated like partnerships for tax purposes, while providing the owners will limited liability as in the case of regular corporations. To qualify as an S-corporation, an entity can have no more than 35 shareholders and only one class of stock. Thus, unlike a limited partnership there is a limit on the number of shareholders. This type of corporation is not suitable when a large number of investors is needed.

Summary
Investors in real estate can enjoy substantial returns, such as sizable cash flows from the rental of the property, attractive tax benefits during the holding period, and substantial capital gains when the real estate is sold. To be sure, real estate has proven an effective hedge against inflation and should be a part of most individuals' investment portfolios. However, there are risks that should be considered. First, high transaction costs may require long holding-periods in many instances; and, property must be actively managed and typically is less liquid than investment in financial assets.

There are several forms of real estate ownership, including sole ownership, tenants in common, joint tenancy, tenancy in its entirety, partnerships, traditional limited partnerships, master limited partnerships, real estate investment trusts, regular corporations, and S-corporations. Each form has distinct advantages and disadvantages, and should be carefully evaluated before entering into.

Chapter 2

Revenue and Expense Characteristics of Real Estate

The relationship between revenues and expenses is an important factor in determining the overall success of a real estate investment. An understanding of the nature of real estate revenues and expenses enables investors to properly evaluate return and ascertain the relative risk associated with a real estate opportunity. This chapter examines the various sources and characteristics of revenue and the expenses associated with real estate investments.

Revenue Sources

With the exception of raw land, the major source of real estate revenue is from income generated by the rental or leasing of property. The amount of income is determined by the type of property, its location, and market conditions. The leasing agreement itself may provide that the lessor share in the tenant's income beyond some initial level or base rent. In these instances, the real estate owner receives a fixed amount of rent each period plus a predetermined percentage of the lessee's income.

Many leasing agreements provide that the lessee share or pay for various operating expenses. For example, if tenants agree to a triple net lease, they are responsible for payment of all expenses associated with maintenance, insurance, and property taxes. If this is the case, the real estate owner's exposure to cost increases is eliminated during the term of the lease. In other instances, the lessee may agree to share with the lessor any increases in specified expenses above a specified level. Although this does not provide total insulation from cost increases, it does reduce the risk somewhat.

Another source of income is the tax savings available to the real estate investor. Investors can reduce their taxes by writing off against income most if not all of their real estate acquisition cost, even though the value of this

13

asset is likely to increase over time. This benefit, called depreciation, is a periodic write-off of the costs of the improvements on a property (e.g., building). Thus, in addition to the various sources of revenue investors in real estate are provided certain benefits unavailable to those who invest in financial assets such as stocks and bonds.

Since depreciation is a noncash expense, it enables investors to generate tax deductions without an additional outlay of funds. Under the recently passed Tax Reform Act of 1986 (TRA) the partnership must depreciate the property under the straight-line method. This noncash expense allows investors to recover their cost over a 27.5-year period in the case of residential properties and 31.5 years for nonresidential properties. The yearly depreciation schedule is determined by the month the asset is placed in service. (Tables 2.1 and 2.2 present the depreciation schedules for residential and nonresidential property respectively.)

Example

Assume that an individual acquires a residential property at a cost of $85,000 (net of any land cost) in June of the current year. To determine his first year depreciation deduction we would merely go to Table 2.1 (since it is residential property) and use the percentage listed under year one and the sixth month (June), 2.0 percent. Following this procedure, the first-year depreciation deduction is $1,700 ($85,000 times 2.0 percent). To determine his depreciation deduction in subsequent years, we would look down the column under month six and multiply the indicated percentage by $85,000. Thus, the depreciation deduction in year two would be $3,060 ($85,000 times 3.6 percent).

Sources of Capital

The various forms of real estate ownership provide opportunities for different degrees of leverage. Leverage occurs when an investor is able to own a property directly, or acquire an equity interest in a property indirectly, using someone else's money. The effect of leverage is twofold: leverage can dramatically enhance the return on a project to an investor, and leverage may dramatically enhance the risk of loss on a project. While risk and return go hand in hand, for many investors the opportunities for leverage traditional in real estate are a primary factor in choosing this type of investment.

Table 2.1 27.5-Year Residential Rental Property (Applicable Percentages)

Recovery Years	Month Placed in Service											
	1	2	3	4	5	6	7	8	9	10	11	12
1	3.5	3.2	2.9	2.6	2.3	2.0	1.7	1.4	1.1	0.8	0.5	0.2
2	3.6	3.6	3.6	3.6	3.6	3.6	3.6	3.6	3.6	3.6	3.6	3.6
3	3.6	3.6	3.6	3.6	3.6	3.6	3.6	3.6	3.6	3.6	3.6	3.6
4	3.6	3.6	3.6	3.6	3.6	3.6	3.6	3.6	3.6	3.6	3.6	3.6
5	3.6	3.6	3.6	3.6	3.6	3.6	3.6	3.6	3.6	3.6	3.6	3.6
6	3.6	3.6	3.6	3.6	3.6	3.6	3.6	3.6	3.6	3.6	3.6	3.6
7	3.6	3.6	3.6	3.6	3.6	3.6	3.6	3.6	3.6	3.6	3.6	3.6
8	3.6	3.6	3.6	3.6	3.6	3.6	3.6	3.6	3.6	3.6	3.6	3.6
9	3.6	3.6	3.6	3.6	3.6	3.6	3.6	3.6	3.6	3.6	3.6	3.6
10	3.6	3.6	3.6	3.6	3.6	3.6	3.6	3.6	3.6	3.6	3.6	3.6
11	3.6	3.6	3.6	3.6	3.6	3.6	3.6	3.6	3.6	3.6	3.6	3.6
12	3.6	3.6	3.6	3.6	3.6	3.6	3.6	3.6	3.6	3.6	3.6	3.6
13	3.6	3.6	3.6	3.6	3.6	3.6	3.6	3.6	3.6	3.6	3.6	3.6
14	3.6	3.6	3.6	3.6	3.6	3.6	3.6	3.6	3.6	3.6	3.6	3.6
15	3.6	3.6	3.6	3.6	3.6	3.6	3.6	3.6	3.6	3.6	3.6	3.6
16	3.6	3.6	3.6	3.6	3.6	3.6	3.6	3.6	3.6	3.6	3.6	3.6
17	3.6	3.6	3.6	3.6	3.6	3.6	3.6	3.6	3.6	3.6	3.6	3.6
18	3.6	3.6	3.6	3.6	3.6	3.6	3.6	3.6	3.6	3.6	3.6	3.6
19	3.6	3.6	3.6	3.6	3.6	3.6	3.6	3.6	3.6	3.6	3.6	3.6
20	3.6	3.6	3.6	3.6	3.6	3.6	3.6	3.6	3.6	3.6	3.6	3.6
21	3.6	3.6	3.6	3.6	3.6	3.6	3.6	3.6	3.6	3.6	3.6	3.6
22	3.6	3.6	3.6	3.6	3.6	3.6	3.6	3.6	3.6	3.6	3.6	3.6
23	3.6	3.6	3.6	3.6	3.6	3.6	3.6	3.6	3.6	3.6	3.6	3.6
24	3.6	3.6	3.6	3.6	3.6	3.6	3.6	3.6	3.6	3.6	3.6	3.6
25	3.6	3.6	3.6	3.6	3.6	3.6	3.6	3.6	3.6	3.6	3.6	3.6
26	3.6	3.6	3.6	3.6	3.6	3.6	3.6	3.6	3.6	3.6	3.6	3.6
27	3.6	3.6	3.6	3.6	3.6	3.6	3.6	3.6	3.6	3.6	3.6	3.6
28	3.6	3.6	3.6	3.6	3.6	3.6	3.6	3.6	3.6	3.6	3.6	3.6
29	2.9	3.2	3.5	3.8	4.1	4.4	1.1	1.4	1.7	2.0	2.3	2.6

Table 2.2 31.5-Year Nonresidential Rental Property (Applicable Percentages)

Recovery Years	Month Placed In Service											
	1	2	3	4	5	6	7	8	9	10	11	12
1	3.0	2.8	2.5	2.2	2.0	1.7	1.5	1.2	0.9	0.7	0.4	0.1
2	3.2	3.2	3.2	3.2	3.2	3.2	3.2	3.2	3.2	3.2	3.2	3.2
3	3.2	3.2	3.2	3.2	3.2	3.2	3.2	3.2	3.2	3.2	3.2	3.2
4	3.2	3.2	3.2	3.2	3.2	3.2	3.2	3.2	3.2	3.2	3.2	3.2
5	3.2	3.2	3.2	3.2	3.2	3.2	3.2	3.2	3.2	3.2	3.2	3.2
6	3.2	3.2	3.2	3.2	3.2	3.2	3.2	3.2	3.2	3.2	3.2	3.2
7	3.2	3.2	3.2	3.2	3.2	3.2	3.2	3.2	3.2	3.2	3.2	3.2
8	3.2	3.2	3.2	3.2	3.2	3.2	3.2	3.2	3.2	3.2	3.2	3.2
9	3.2	3.2	3.2	3.2	3.2	3.2	3.2	3.2	3.2	3.2	3.2	3.2
10	3.2	3.2	3.2	3.2	3.2	3.2	3.2	3.2	3.2	3.2	3.2	3.2
11	3.2	3.2	3.2	3.2	3.2	3.2	3.2	3.2	3.2	3.2	3.2	3.2
12	3.2	3.2	3.2	3.2	3.2	3.2	3.2	3.2	3.2	3.2	3.2	3.2
13	3.2	3.2	3.2	3.2	3.2	3.2	3.2	3.2	3.2	3.2	3.2	3.2
14	3.2	3.2	3.2	3.2	3.2	3.2	3.2	3.2	3.2	3.2	3.2	3.2
15	3.2	3.2	3.2	3.2	3.2	3.2	3.2	3.2	3.2	3.2	3.2	3.2
16	3.2	3.2	3.2	3.2	3.2	3.2	3.2	3.2	3.2	3.2	3.2	3.2
17	3.2	3.2	3.2	3.2	3.2	3.2	3.2	3.2	3.2	3.2	3.2	3.2
18	3.2	3.2	3.2	3.2	3.2	3.2	3.2	3.2	3.2	3.2	3.2	3.2
19	3.2	3.2	3.2	3.2	3.2	3.2	3.2	3.2	3.2	3.2	3.2	3.2
20	3.2	3.2	3.2	3.2	3.2	3.2	3.2	3.2	3.2	3.2	3.2	3.2
21	3.2	3.2	3.2	3.2	3.2	3.2	3.2	3.2	3.2	3.2	3.2	3.2
22	3.2	3.2	3.2	3.2	3.2	3.2	3.2	3.2	3.2	3.2	3.2	3.2
23	3.2	3.2	3.2	3.2	3.2	3.2	3.2	3.2	3.2	3.2	3.2	3.2
24	3.2	3.2	3.2	3.2	3.2	3.2	3.2	3.2	3.2	3.2	3.2	3.2
25	3.2	3.2	3.2	3.2	3.2	3.2	3.2	3.2	3.2	3.2	3.2	3.2
26	3.2	3.2	3.2	3.2	3.2	3.2	3.2	3.2	3.2	3.2	3.2	3.2
27	3.2	3.2	3.2	3.2	3.2	3.2	3.2	3.2	3.2	3.2	3.2	3.2
28	3.2	3.2	3.2	3.2	3.2	3.2	3.2	3.2	3.2	3.2	3.2	3.2
29	3.2	3.2	3.2	3.2	3.2	3.2	3.2	3.2	3.2	3.2	3.2	3.2
30	3.2	3.2	3.2	3.2	3.2	3.2	3.2	3.2	3.0	3.2	3.2	3.2
31	3.2	3.2	3.2	3.2	3.2	3.2	2.4	2.7	0.1	3.2	3.2	3.2
32	3.0	1.2	1.5	1.7	2.0	2.3	0.1	0.1		0.1	3.2	3.2
33											0.4	0.7

Conventional Financing

In acquiring real estate, investors gain possession of a property that may serve as collateral for a loan, effectively reducing their investment basis. An individual, partnership, or corporation may obtain a mortgage on a property. Shares in a master limited partnership, REIT, or corporation may be bought on margin.

The willingness of a lender to advance capital to an investor depends on some combination of (1) the creditworthiness of the investor, (2) the capacity of the investor to repay, (3) the anticipated proceeds of the investment, and (4) the value of the property itself. Conventional sources of financing include commercial banks, insurance companies, mortgage companies, insurance companies and pension funds. As conventional lenders frequently take a more conservative view of these factors than investors do, investors are frequently in a position where they are struggling to acquire enough capital to make an investment viable. This problem has been made more difficult for investors by two things: the recent trend of banks packaging their loans for the secondary market, which requires them to adhere to strict qualifying standards, and the increased regulatory scrutiny that has followed in the wake of a number of highly-publicized bank failures.

In general, the market for loanable funds is quite competitive. An investor with a good project will benefit from shopping conventional lenders. Investors frequently encounter a surprising variety of terms and rates. Conventional lenders are increasingly using variable-rate loans, equity-participation loans, and a variety of balloon structures to help meet investors' needs.

Creative Financing

Creative financing involves obtaining funds from nonconventional sources. The most frequent source of nonconventional financing is the seller of the property. In situations where sellers have a problem moving their property at the desired price, investors have an opportunity to use some of the sellers' equity as a source of capital. This situation might arise in a slow market, where the property has undesirable features, or when the seller has an unrealistic view of the property's value. In utilizing this source of capital, investors must carefully weigh the costs and benefits of the project in accordance with the principles developed in Chapter 5. The effective use of this source of capital is complex, but it may make the difference between a project that is viable and one that is not.

Example

Consider an apartment in a deteriorated neighborhood. Despite a good gross rent multiplier and favorable cash flow, it has not moved because it looks unattractive. The present owner values the apartment at $200,000, but it has been on the market a year at that price. The investor values it at $150,000, and the most any conventional source of capital will lend on it is $120,000. The investor calculates a true rate of return on her investment of 18 percent if she purchases it for $150,000 and secures a conventional mortgage of $120,000 at 12 percent. If she purchases it for $200,000 and invests $80,000 of her own money in it, her internal rate of return falls to 4 percent. However, the investor may propose to the seller that she will pay the full price of $200,000 for the property if the seller will take back a second mortgage for $120,000 at 6 percent. The investor can then take a first mortgage from conventional sources for $60,000 at 12 percent. Although the investor has paid a higher price for the property, her total finance costs have fallen, her depreciation basis is larger, and her initial investment is smaller. The combined effect of these changes may well increase the return on the project to over 18 percent!

Real Estate Expenses

Real estate expenses are incurred during the acquisition, holding, and disposal phases. These costs vary depending upon the type of real estate, its location, and general market conditions.

Acquisition Period Expenses

During the acquisition phase, costs associated with property appraisal, surveys, credit checks, debt financing (including title insurance and mortgage origination fees and points), inspection and various legal fees will most likely be incurred by the buyer. Additionally, depending upon bargaining power, the buyer may be required to share in transfer taxes, documentary stamps as well as additional fees.

In the event that the buyer finances the purchase with debt, he or she may be required to pay "points" at time of settlement. A point represents one percent of the amount of funds borrowed. This enables the lender to receive higher yields by requiring the borrower to pay a portion of the interest up front. The number of points charged by the lender varies depending on the borrower's relationship with the lending institution, the attractiveness of the project, and general market conditions.

Holding Phase Expenses

During the holding phase the owner's expenses may include leasing fees, management fees, utilities and maintenance expenses, marketing costs, insurance expenses, and property taxes, as well as administrative fees such as legal and accounting expenses. These expenses vary depending upon the type of real estate investment.

When real estate is purchased, only part of its cost is usually composed of the investor's capital. The remainder of the required funds are generally secured through debt. In fact, often 80 percent or more of acquisition costs are financed with debt. Thus, borrowing plays an important role in real estate investing. The borrowing of funds creates two important obligations. First, the borrower must pay the lender interest on the funds borrowed. Second, the borrower must pay back the loan. It is important that one fully understands the essential conditions of the loan as it relates to these two commitments.

In regard to the first obligation, the terms of the interest rate requirement must be examined. Broadly speaking, interest rates may either be fixed or floating. Fixed-rate financing means that the rate of interest does not vary over the term of the loan. A floating loan, on the other hand, is tied to an index, such as the prime rate or 90-day treasury bill rate. Payments are adjusted periodically, usually on either a quarterly or yearly basis.

Fixed-Rate Financing. Under fixed-rate financing, the risk associated with changing interest rates falls largely upon the lender. If rates rise, the lender will miss the opportunity of lending at a higher rate. If rates fall, the borrower may be able to refinance at these lower rates.

Variable-Rate Financing. With floating rates, the lender's interest charges are adjusted to enable him to realize current yields. The borrower is at the mercy of market rate fluctuations. Due to these factors, fixed-rate financing alternatives will at first cost more than its variable-, or floating-, rate counterpart. However, under variable-rate financing the borrower is fully exposed to rising interest rates and may find this method of financing more costly in the long run.

The second obligation, the repayment of the loan principal, may be accomplished in many ways. Sometimes a lender will not require repayment until the end of the loan term, this is referred to as a balloon payment. Usually the lender requires periodic repayment of the loan, commonly called amortization. This can be accomplished by requiring that the borrower either make equal principal payments or make level payments over the life of the loan. In the first case, the total payment decreases over the life of the loan as the size of the outstanding balance diminishes. Under the latter arrangement, the total payments are constant, but the principal payments increase over the life of the loan while the interest payments decrease by a like amount so that total payments remain level.

In addition, the lender may be willing to amortize the loan over a long period but require total payment within this amortization period. For example, a commercial loan may call for a steady payment with a 30-year amortization. However, it may contain a balloon feature which may require the borrower to repay the entire loan at the end of, say, five years, while still figuring the payments until then based on a 30-year amortization schedule. The advantage in combining a long amortization with a balloon payment is that borrowers know what their debt requirements will be, and the lender has not locked them into a fixed rate for a prolonged period. At the balloon payment date, borrowers can either renegotiate the terms of the loan or refinance it through another source. Borrowers run the risk that rates will be higher at that time or that they will not be able to refinance the loan at all.

The maximum length of the repayment period will be influenced by the expected life of the asset to be financed, general credit conditions, and the financial strength of the borrower. Furthermore, government agencies, in an effort to make low-income housing more attractive to investors, have in the past offered 40-year or longer mortgages.

Participation Loans. The participation loan has gained popularity over the past few years. Typically, borrowers are provided with loans below the market rate, with amortization periods similar to those available with ordinary fixed-rate financing. These loans might be priced at two percent below prevailing rates. Under these arrangements, the lender is also entitled to a certain percent of cash flow from operations, profit from refinancing, and/or sale of the assets.

There are advantages and disadvantages in participation loans for both the borrower and the lender. From the borrower's perspective, the loan repayment requirements would be less burdensome. However, the upside potential is somewhat limited, since the lender shares in the project's success. The lender, in turn, would have the opportunity of sharing in the profits of the venture without taking on the risk of ownership. However, if the project is marginal, the lender would have committed funds to a project in which the return is less than that otherwise available in the marketplace.

Zero-Coupon Debt Instruments. An increasing number of real estate investments involve the use of zero-coupon debt instruments, which require that both principal and interest be paid when the debt matures. The zero-coupon feature allows the borrower to conserve the cash that would otherwise be used to service debt. While this feature may lessen the borrower's cash requirements during the life of the loan, it requires a sizable cash drain when the debt is paid and increases the borrower's risk.

In these cases, the borrower must determine whether the appreciation of the real estate will be sufficient to allow for refinancing of the debt. The investor must ascertain whether the proceeds are sufficient to provide sufficient funds to pay off the debt, as well as the tax liability, and still provide an acceptable after-tax return.

Liability. In addition to the liens placed directly on the properties to be financed, lenders often require borrowers to be personally liable. Recourse financing simply means that, in the event that a note is in default, the lender can secure the delinquent payments from the borrowers directly.

Nonrecourse financing requires no personal backing, and the lender has no recourse if the obligations are not satisfied by the properties pledged as collateral. In this instance, the borrower would not be required to personally guarantee the loan. The lender's risk may be greater under nonrecourse financing, and the borrower may therefore be required to pay a higher rate of interest.

The owner of real estate can also expect to pay income taxes on any profits realized during this period of time. These taxes will be based on the amount of income and the form in which the real estate is held.

Disposal Phase Expenses
The owner of real estate will experience significant expenses during disposal phase. For example, selling commissions are normally incurred in disposing of the property. In addition there may be prepayment penalties associated with mortgages on the property. Other expenses such as legal costs, transfer taxes and stamps as well as fees associated with transferring title are to be expected. Finally, to the extent that there is any gain resulting from the sale of real estate, the seller incurs both federal and state income tax liabilities.

Summary

The investor may realize a significant amount of income by holding real estate. The amount of income is a function of the revenue and expense characteristics of the properties held. Various expenses are incurred during the acquisition, holding, and disposal phase. During the acquisition phase, various fees include transfer taxes, appraisals, documentary stamps, and mortgage point charges. During the holding phase these costs include administrative, operating, and financial expenses. Administrative expenses may include legal and accounting costs, while operating expenses may include costs associated with maintenance, leasing, and insurance, as well as property and income taxes. If the investor borrows money, interest expense is incurred.

In addition to the amount of debt, other characteristics of the loan are very important. Among these are the interest rate requirements and the repayment requirement. The interest rate on a debt instrument may be of a fixed or a variable nature. Depending on the type, certain interest-rate risks are borne by either the lender or borrower. In some instances, the arrangement may be of a participating nature, which entitles the lender to share in a predetermined amount of project profits in return for accepting a lower interest rate for the borrowed funds.

Finally, the disposal phase generally requires the seller to incur commission costs, legal fees, as well as taxes on any gain realized from the sale of the property.

Chapter 3

Evaluating Real Estate Financial Statements

A proper evaluation of real estate investment requires that the investor has a thorough understanding of the financial statements. The two most important statements, the income statement and the cash flow statement, are examined in depth in this chapter. It is important to realize that one cannot evaluate an investment using one statement in isolation. While an income statement provides information about the tax implications of a real estate investment, it will not be a good indicator of value by itself.

For example, a real estate investment could show profit over a period of time yet drain the participant of cash. On the other hand, a real estate investment could show losses over time yet generate significant yearly cash flow to its owner. In the latter instance, the investor is likely to have both sizable cash flow and reduced taxes. Thus, the investment's cash flow net of taxes is a better indicator of real estate's true worth. Thus, these two statements must be viewed collectively in order to gain proper insight as to the desirability of the investment.

Income Statements

The income statement for accounting or tax purposes reports the results of operations over a given period. Essentially, this statement compares the real estate investment's revenues with its expenses. If revenues exceed expenses, the investment will show a profit. On the other hand, if expenses exceed revenues, a loss for the period will result.

A real estate investment's income statement may report low profits. At first glance, this comparison of a real estate project's revenues and expenses may seem misleading. A closer inspection would probably reveal that some of the expenses that cause a low profit on the income statement are noncash in nature. Such items represent accounting charges against expenditures made in the past that did not require current cash outlays.

25

Depreciation is an excellent example of such a noncash expense. As mentioned in Chapter 2, taxpayers who purchase certain real estate assets are permitted to charge off their costs over a prescribed period of time. This yearly charge, called depreciation, is a deduction that is the result of a prior purchase of an asset and thus involves no cash outlay at the time depreciation is taken. For tax purposes, however, it is a deductible item. This and other noncash items enable investors to show lower profits on their tax returns, while at the same time benefiting from potential tax-free cash distributions.

Suppose an investor has an opportunity to purchase rental property costing $100,000 (see 27.5-year depreciation schedule). Thus he or she is entitled to receive deductions up to 3.5 percent (of the cost of the building) or $90,000 ($100,000 less $10,000 land cost) the first year. Suppose further that the investor puts up the entire $100,000 and that rental income from this investment is expected to be $18,000 per year. Operating expenses are estimated as follows: leasing expense of $1,800 per year, maintenance costs $1,000 per year, insurance $300, and property taxes $1,200. Table 3.1 represents the investor's income statement for the first year of this investment.

Table 3.1 Income Statement for the Year Ended 19X1

Rental income	**$18,000**
Less:	
Leasing expense	1,800
Maintenance	1,000
Insurance	300
Property taxes	1,200
Depreciation expense	3,150
Profit	$10,550
Tax liability (28%)	$ 2,954

Table 3.1 shows that this investment results in a pre-tax profit of $10,550 the first year. If the investor's marginal tax rate is 28 percent, the first year's tax liability is $2,954 (the profit times the investor's marginal tax rate). If the investor were in the 15-percent tax bracket, the tax liability would only be $1,583.

Cash Flow Statements

Table 3.2 shows the cash flow statement for the working example. While the investment has taxable income of $10,550, it generates $13,700 in cash flow. The difference between the cash flow ($13,700) and the taxable income ($10,550) is the $3,150 depreciation expense contained in the income statement. Thus, while depreciation reduces the amount of taxable income it has no affect on the investor's cash flow since it is a noncash expense.

Table 3.2 Cash Flow Statement for the Year Ended 19X1

Rental income	$18,000
Less:	
Leasing expense	1,800
Maintenance	1,000
Insurance	300
Property taxes	1,200
Cash flow	$13,700

The investment's current yield after tax liability is $10,746 (i.e., $13,700 of cash flow less the $2,954 of tax liability). The return on invested capital in year one would be 10.746 percent ($10,746/$100,000).

Impact of Debt

Now let's consider the impact of debt on the investor's first-year income and cash flow statements. Suppose that the investor puts up $20,000 and borrows the remainder ($80,000) over a 30-year period (assuming standard amortization) at an interest rate of 10 percent per annum. Table 3.3 lists the interest, principal, debt service, and the remaining balance for each of the 30 years that the investor's loan is in existence.

The revised income statement in Table 3.4 shown how the investor's borrowing of $80,000 over a 30-year term affects the income and cash flow statements.

Table 3.3 $80,000 Loan Amortization Schedule
             (30-Year Loan at 10 Percent)

Year	Total Interest	Total Principal	Debt Service	Remaining Balance
1	$ 7,979.97	$ 444.75	$ 8,424.72	$79,555.24
2	7,933.40	491.32	8,424.72	79,063.91
3	7,881.98	542.74	8,424.72	78,521.18
4	7,825.12	599.60	8,424.72	77,921.57
5	7,772.36	662.36	8,424.72	77,259.21
6	7,692.98	731.74	8,424.72	76,527.47
7	7,616.35	808.37	8,424.72	75,719.11
8	7,531.69	893.03	8,424.72	74,826.09
9	7,438.20	986.52	8,424.72	73,839.57
10	7,334.91	1,089.81	8,424.72	72,749.77
11	7,220.79	1,203.93	8,424.72	71,545.84
12	7,094.72	1,330.00	8,424.72	70,215.84
13	6,955.46	1,469.26	8,424.72	68,746.58
14	6,801.60	1,623.12	8,424.72	67,123.45
15	6,631.64	1,793.08	8,424.72	65,330.38
16	6,443.88	1,980.84	8,424.72	63,349.53
17	6,236.45	2,188.27	8,424.72	61,161.26
18	6,007.33	2,417.39	8,424.72	58,743.87
19	5,754.18	2,670.54	8,424.72	56,073.33
20	5,474.54	2,950.18	8,424.72	53,123.15
21	5,165.61	3,259.11	8,424.72	49,864.04
22	4,824.36	3,600.36	8,424.72	46,263.68
23	4,447.34	3,977.38	8,424.72	42,286.29
24	4,030.85	4,393.87	8,424.72	37,892.41
25	3,570.76	4,853.96	8,424.72	33,038.45
26	3,062.50	5,362.22	8,424.72	27,676.23
27	2,501.01	5,923.71	8,424.72	21,752.52
28	1,880.70	6,544.02	8,424.72	15,208.50
29	1,195.48	7,229.24	8,424.72	7,979.26
30	438.48	7,979.26	8,417.74	0

Table 3.4 Income Statement—Leveraged (for the Year Ended 19X1)

Rental income	$18,000
Less:	
Leasing expense	1,800
Maintenance	1,000
Insurance	300
Property taxes	1,200
Depreciation expense	3,150
Interest expense	7,980
Profit	$2,570
Tax liability (28%)	$ 720

Table 3.4 demonstrates that the investor's leveraged investment results in a taxable income of $2,570 for the first year versus $10,954 under the unleveraged scenario. Note that profits are decreased by the amount of interest expense, or $7,980 ($10,550 minus $2,570). Given the investor's marginal tax rate of 28 percent, this decrease in first-year profits results in a reduction in tax liability to $720. Thus the net tax savings due to the inclusion of the interest expense deduction is $2,234 ($2,954 less $720).

In addition to the decreased first-year profits associated with borrowing, the investor's leveraged investment continues to provide a positive cash flow. The initial year's cash flow statement would be as follows:

Table 3.5 Cash Flow Statement—Leveraged (for the Year Ended 19X1)

Rental income	$18,000
Less:	
Leasing expense	1,800
Maintenance	1,000
Insurance	300
Property taxes	1,200
Debt payment	8,425
Cash flow	$ 5,275

By utilizing leverage, the investor's total first year's return would now be $4,555 (the $5,275 of cash flow less taxes due of $720). The first year's return on equity would be 22.775 percent ($4,555/$20,000) versus percent 10.746 ($10,746/$100,000) under the unleveraged scenario.

Thus, in this instance, the investment becomes more attractive with the introduction of leverage. By borrowing $80,000, the investor benefits from deducting interest charges, whereas he or she would have obtained fewer tax benefits without the additional benefit of leverage.

The impact of the interaction of noncash expenses and taxes on the investor's rate of return can be seen more dramatically when the investment does not earn a conventional accounting profit. This is shown by assuming the example developed in Tables 3.4 and 3.5 but with the change that the investor realizes a lower level of rental income, say $14,000. Table 3.6 presents the revised income statement, assuming that rental income drops from $18,000 to $14,000.

Table 3.6 Income Statement—Leveraged (for the Year Ended 19X1)

Rental income	*$14,000*
Less:	
Leasing expense	1,800
Maintenance	1,000
Insurance	400
Property taxes	1,200
Depreciation expense	3,150
Interest expense	7,980
Profit (loss)	$(1,430)
Tax savings (28%)	400

A drop in the rental income for the leveraged property from $18,000 to $14,000 results in the loss of $1,430 as shown indicated in Table 3.6. In the case where the investor is in the 28-percent tax bracket and has less than $100,000 of income, this loss produces a tax saving of $400.40 ($1,430 × .28).

Table 3.7 illustrates the impact of the lower rental income figure on the investment's cash flow.

Table 3.7 Cash Flow Statement—Leveraged (for the Year Ended 19X1)

Rental income	$14,000
Less:	
Leasing expense	1,800
Maintenance	1,000
Insurance	300
Property taxes	1,200
Debt payment	8,425
Cash flow	$1,275

The cash flow from the investment is still positive. As a result of eliminating noncash expenditures and allowing for payment of principal as well as interest, Table 3.7 reveals a positive cash flow of $1,275. This circumstance still yields the investor an actual first-year return of $1,675.40 (cash flow of $1,275 plus tax savings of $400.40) or a return of 8.377 percent on an investment of $20,000.

This does not measure the total return on the investment. To this must be added the increase in principal and whatever appreciation occurs. Calculating the total return is examined in the next chapter. However, abstracting from risk, it should be clear that greater cash flows and leverage can interact to produce a very favorable return to the investor under current tax law.

The immediate impact of leverage is quite clear in terms of its impact on taxable income and cash flow. Not as clear is the investment's future prospects due to leverage. Although the debt service requirements (dollar amount of payments) are constant, their composition is not. Specifically, deductible interest charges fall over time, subjecting the investor to greater tax exposure as more and more of the yearly debt servicing requirements are composed of principal repayments. Hence, interest deductions in subsequent years decrease with the use of debt financing.

To examine the net cash flow of the investment over a ten-year period, consider this example. Assume that rental income equals $18,000 and expenses are the same as before (as found in Tables 3.1 and 3.2) and that the amortization schedule is the same as the one in Table 3.4.

To determine the net cash flows, first determine the investor's tax liability. Table 3.8 presents the income statements over the ten-year period. The last line of each year's income statement represents the investor's tax liability,

Table 3.8 Income Statement—Real Estate Project

Year	1	2	3	4
Rental income	$18,000	$18,000	$18,000	$18,000
Less:				
Leasing expense	1,800	1,800	1,800	1,800
Maintenance	1,000	1,000	1,000	1,000
Insurance	300	300	300	300
Property taxes	1,200	1,200	1,200	1,200
Interest expense	7,980	7,933	7,882	7,825
Depreciation expense	3,150	3,240	3,240	3,240
Profit	$ 2,570	$ 2,527	$ 2,578	$ 2,635
Tax liability (28%)	$ 720	$ 708	$ 722	$ 738

Year	5	6	7	8
Rental income	$18,000	$18,000	$18,000	$18,000
Less:				
Leasing expense	1,800	1,800	1,800	1,800
Maintenance	1,000	1,000	1,000	1,000
Insurance	300	300	300	300
Property taxes	1,200	1,200	1,200	1,200
Interest expense	7,772	7,693	7,616	7,532
Depreciation expense	3,240	3,240	3,240	3,240
Profit	$ 2,688	$ 2,767	$ 2,844	$ 2,928
Tax liability (28%)	$ 753	$ 775	$ 796	$ 820

Year	9	10
Rental income	$18,000	$18,000
Less:		
Leasing expense	1,800	1,800
Maintenance	1,000	1,000
Insurance	300	300
Property taxes	1,200	1,200
Interest expense	7,438	7,335
Depreciation expense	3,240	3,240
Profit	$ 3,022	$ 3,125
Tax liability (28%)	$ 846	$ 875

which is found by multiplying the profit by the investor's marginal tax rate. (This example assumes a marginal tax rate of 28 percent.) As shown in Table 3.8, the investor's tax liability gradually increases over the period. This increase in exposure to taxes is a result of the lower interest expenses incurred as more principal has been paid off.

The next step in determining the amount of yearly net cash flow is the development of cash flow statements. Since in this example the revenues, expenses, and debt servicing requirements remain constant, the cash flows for all ten years would be the same as in year one. Table 3.9 depicts the annual cash flow statement for the investment.

As shown in Table 3.9 the investor experiences annual cash flows of $5,275 during the initial ten-year period. However, as seen in Table 3.8 the investor is also liable for taxes on income during this period. Table 3.10 reports the net cash flow to the investor over the ten-year period. Column 2 represents the investment's cash flow as calculated in table 3.9, while column 3 represents the investor's tax liability as calculated in Table 3.8. Column 4 represents the investor's net cash flow and is found by subtracting the yearly tax liability (3), from the expected yearly cash flow (2).

The decision to purchase the property would depend not only on the investment's expected after-tax cash flows but on its likely appreciation potential as well. Under the leveraged alternative, the investor's initial cash investment is greatly reduced ($20,000 versus $100,000), as is the annual cash flow, due to the servicing requirements of the debt.

Table 3.9 Cash Flow Statement—Real Estate Project

Rental income	*$18,000*
Less:	
Leasing expense	1,800
Maintenance	1,000
Insurance	300
Property taxes	1,200
Debt payment	8,425
Cash flow	$ 5,275

Table 3.10 Net Cash Flows—Real Estate Project

(1) Year	(2) Cash Flow	(3) Tax Liability	(4) (2) — (3) Net Cash Flow
1	$5,275	$ 720	$4,555
2	5,275	708	4,567
3	5,275	722	4,553
4	5,275	738	4,537
5	5,275	753	4,522
6	5,275	775	4,500
7	5,275	796	4,479
8	5,275	820	4,455
9	5,275	846	4,429
10	5,275	875	4,400
Totals:	$52,750	$ 7,753	$44,997

Impact of Varying the Amortization Period

The illustration just considered assumed a mortgage amortization of 30 years. The 30-year term resulted in only $444.75 of the $8,424.72 in debt service going to principal reduction in the first year. Furthermore, interest charges exceed principal payments during the first 23 years of the 30-year loan. However, as time passes the amount of interest relative to the principal payments diminishes, therefore the cash requirements remain constant over the 30-year loan, while the tax deductions (interest expense) decrease over the life of the loan.

The relative proportion of interest and principal at any given time is determined by the length of the amortization and by the effective interest rate. The longer the term of the loan and the higher the interest rate, the greater the proportion of the interest expense to the total debt service requirement.

We will reexamine the real estate project, using a 15-year amortization period instead of the 30-year amortization period used earlier. Table 3.11 lists the interest, principal, debt service, and the remaining balance for each of the 15 years that the investor's loan is in existence. The revised income statements for the 10-year period (Table 3.12) illustrate effect of the investor's borrowing of $80,000 over a 15-year term.

Table 3.11 $80,000 Loan Amortization Schedule
(15-Year Loan at 10 Percent)

Year	Total Interest	Total Principal	Debt Service	Remaining Balance
1	$7,890.85	$2,425.31	$10,316.16	$77,574.70
2	7,636.89	2,679.27	10,316.16	74,895.43
3	7,356.33	2,959.83	10,316.16	71,935.60
4	7,046.38	3,269.78	10,316.16	68,665.82
5	6,704.00	3,612.16	10,316.16	65,053.66
6	6,325.77	3,990.39	10,316.16	61,063.26
7	5,907.92	4,408.24	10,316.16	56,655.02
8	5,446.32	4,869.84	10,316.16	51,785.18
9	4,936.38	5,379.78	10,316.16	46,405.40
10	4,373.05	5,943.11	0,316.16	40,462.29
11	3,750.71	6,565.45	10,316.16	33,896.84
12	3,063.22	7,252.94	10,316.16	26,643.90
13	2,303.75	8,012.41	10,316.16	18,631.49
14	1,464.75	8,851.41	10,316.16	9,780.08
15	537.90	9,780.08	10,317.98	0

The 15-year loan requires a larger yearly principal repayment and a lower yearly interest expense relative to the 30-year loan. As shown in Table 3.12, each year's profits and corresponding tax liability is greater than that under the 30-year mortgage scenario.

Table 3.13 depicts the annual cash flow statement for the investment assuming 15-year debt amortization. All cash flow items are the same as before except for the debt payment, which is $10,316 under the 15-year loan the annual debt servicing requirement, versus only $8,425 under the 30-year scenario. The annual cash flow is $3,384, versus $5,275 under the 30-year plan. Thus, the shorter amortization period results in $1,891 (i.e., $5,275 minus $3,384) reduced cash flow each year.

Table 3.14 compares the net cash flows (yearly cash flows less tax liabilities) of the 30-year and 15-year mortgages. Column 2 represents the net cash flow under the 30-year scenario as calculated in Table 3.10, while column 3 represents the net cash flow under the 15-year scenario developed in Tables 3.12 and 3.13. Column 4 represents the investor's net cash flow advantage with the 30-year amortization period and is found by subtracting column 3 from column 2.

Table 3.12 Income Statement—Real Estate Project

Year	1	2	3	4
Rental income	$18,000	$18,000	$18,000	$18,000
Less:				
Leasing expense	1,800	1,800	1,800	1,800
Maintenance	1,000	1,000	1,000	1,000
Insurance	300	300	300	300
Property taxes	1,200	1,200	1,200	1,200
Interest expense	7,891	7,637	7,356	7,046
Depreciation expense	3,150	3,240	3,240	3,240
Profit	$ 2,659	$ 2,823	$ 3,104	$ 3,414
Tax liability (28%)	$1,052	$1,158	$1,275	$1,404

Year	5	6	7	8
Rental income	$18,000	$18,000	$18,000	$18,000
Less:				
Leasing expense	1,800	1,800	1,800	1,800
Maintenance	1,000	1,000	1,000	1,000
Insurance	300	300	300	300
Property taxes	1,200	1,200	1,200	1,200
Interest expense	6,704	6,326	5,908	5,446
Depreciation expense	3,240	3,240	3,240	3,240
Profit	$ 3,756	$ 4,134	$ 4,552	$ 5,014
Tax liability (28%)	$ 1,052	$ 1,158	$ 1,275	$ 1,404

Year	9	10
Rental income	$18,000	$18,000
Less:		
Leasing expense	1,800	1,800
Maintenance	1,000	1,000
Insurance	300	300
Property taxes	1,200	1,200
Interest expense	4,936	4,373
Depreciation expense	3,240	3,240
Profit	$ 5,524	$ 6,087
Tax liability (28%)	$ 1,547	$ 1,704

Table 3.13 Cash Flow Statement—Real Estate Project

Rental income	$18,000
Less:	
Leasing expense	1,800
Maintenance	1,000
Insurance	300
Property taxes	1,200
Debt payment	10,316
Cash flow	$ 3,384

As shown in Table 3.14, the 30-year amortization period mortgage provides the investor with $22,657 of additional total net cash flow over the 10-year period compared with the 15-year amortization period mortgage. This is due to the 30-year mortgage's lower annual payments and lower tax liability.

Table 3.14 Comparison of Net Cash Flows—15-Year Mortgage versus 30-Year Mortgage

Period	30-Year Amortization	5-Year Amortization	Yearly Cash Advantage 30-Year Amortization
1	$4,555	$2,639	$1,916
2	4,567	2,594	1,973
3	4,553	2,515	2,038
4	4,537	2,428	2,109
5	4,522	2,332	2,190
6	4,500	2,226	2,274
7	4,479	2,109	2,370
8	4,455	1,980	2,475
9	4,429	1,837	2,592
10	4,400	1,680	2,720
Totals:	$44,997	$22,340	$22,657

The 30-year mortgage is more attractive in terms of both annual cash flow and tax liabilities. Another factor must be considered: after the tenth year of the 30-year mortgage, the investor is left with a mortgage balance of

72,749.77 (see Table 3.3). Under the 15-year mortgage, the investor's mortgage balance is only $40,462.29 at the end of year 10 (see Table 3.11).

By choosing the 30-year mortgage, the investor has a remaining balance of $32,287.48 ($72,749.77 minus $40,462.29) more than under the 15-year term. The investor must weigh the additional funds required during the disposal phase with the benefits of additional net cash flow ($22,657) during the real estate's holding period.

Summary

As an investment, real estate may have tax advantages as well as economic value. These investments typically experience low taxable profits in the initial years. As such, they also have the ability to generate and distribute sizable amounts of cash tax free. The ability to generate deductions while providing cash-free distributions is one of the key features of many real estate investments.

Investors need to know the difference between an investment's accounting profits and its cash flow characteristics in order to understand the mechanics of the workings of real estate investments. The introduction of leverage allows the investor to increase after-tax returns while limiting invested capital. The investor must view the cash flow and tax effects over the life of the investment, since the use of debt as a tax shield diminishes over time.

Chapter 4

Tax Implications for Real Estate Investing

One of the many reasons real estate has been a very popular investment is that it can provide investors with after-tax returns substantially higher than those attained through investing in financial assets such as stocks and bonds. This is because investors are entitled to tax benefits that enable them to reduce their current tax exposure, and therefore increase their yield from real estate activities.

The real value of any investment is based on the after-tax return it provides investors. Investors' after-tax return is directly influenced by the mix of revenues and expenses as well as the type of expenses (cash versus noncash) generated by the investment. Likewise, real estate investors' marginal tax rate has an effect on their after-tax return. Changes in any of these variables affect investors' after-tax rate of return. This chapter examines the current tax law as it relates to investment decisions.

Classification of Income

The Tax Reform Act of 1986 categorized income as being active, portfolio, or passive. *Active income* includes wages, salaries, and other sources of income that result from an individual providing services; *portfolio income* includes interest and dividend income; and *passive income* comes from activities in which the taxpayer did not materially participate. This classification scheme was devised to eliminate the use of passive losses as a means of reducing tax liability. In particular, losses generated from real estate activities where investors do not materially participate are categorized as passive losses and therefore cannot be used to offset wages or portfolio income.

Investors who partake in passive real estate activities after the Tax Reform Act's enactment generally can only apply their share of these losses against other passive income. Thus, they will not be allowed to apply these losses against earned or portfolio income.

The Tax Reform Act of 1986 provided transition rules for those who purchased shelter-oriented passive investments prior to December 31, 1986. For these investors, the passive loss rules will be phased in over a period of four years. When this provision takes full affect (1991), losses generated from investing in pre-1987 passive activities will only be allowed to offset other passive income. Table 4.1 presents the yearly phase-in schedule.

The Tax Reform Act of 1986 did provide some relief to real estate investors. Taxpayers with adjusted gross incomes of less than $100,000 and who are actively involved in real estate activities can deduct up to $25,000 in losses against active income. For taxpayers with adjusted gross incomes above $100,000, the allowance is reduced by 50 percent of the amount of the losses. For individuals with adjusted gross incomes above $150,000, the losses are treated as passive for tax purposes.

Table 4.1   Passive Losses Phase-In Schedule

Taxable Year	Percentage Allowed
1986	100%
1987	65%
1988	40%
1989	20%
1990	10%
1991 and thereafter	0%

Note: The phase-in provision affects only those individuals who entered into shelter-oriented activities prior to 1987.

Individual and Corporate Tax Rates

The Tax Reform Act of 1986 reduced income tax rates for both individuals and corporations, and eliminated the distinction between ordinary income and capital gains tax rates. This has great significance for evaluating the use of real estate as an investment. Prior to this recent tax legislation, the desirability of investing in and holding real estate was affected by the fact that for many individuals in the higher tax brackets ordinary income from investments was taxed at a higher rate than the gains realized from holding property for longer than six months. The effect of these changes was to enhance short- and medium-term real estate investments relative to longer-term investments. This change also influenced the desirability of different types of real estate investments, generally favoring those investments with depreciation expenses over those with long-term appreciation potential.

Like-Kind Exchanges

Section 1031 of the Internal Revenue Code provides that under certain circumstances the owner of real property can exchange that property for other like-kind property without recognition of a gain or loss on the transaction. In order to avoid this recognition, the exchange must only be a property-for-property swap. In cases where in addition to property, cash or another form of "boot" is exchanged, the receiver of "boot" is required to recognize a portion of the gain but limited to the amount of boot received.

Individual and Corporate Tax Rates

Table 4.2 presents the 1990 tax rate schedule of single taxpayers and married couples filing joint returns based on taxable income. Taxable income is based on the taxpayers' total income, any adjustments to total income, as well as other factors such as itemized deductions and exemptions.

Table 4.2 Individual Tax Rates on Taxable Income—1990 Tax Brackets

Single Filer	Married Couples Filing Jointly	Tax Rate
up to $19,450	up to $32,450	15%
$19,450 to $47,050	$32,450 to $78,400	28%
$47,050 to $97,620	$78,400 to $185,000	33% (surcharge)

Note: the 33% marginal rate represents a 5% surcharge designed to eliminate the benefits of the 15% rate. Once those benefits are eliminated, the marginal tax rate reverts to 28%.

Table 4.3 presents the 1988 tax rate schedule of corporate taxpayers.

Table 4.3 Corporate Tax Rates on Taxable Income—1988 Tax Brackets

Taxable Income	Marginal Tax Rate
up to $50,000	15%
$50,001 to $75,000	25
$75,001 to $100,000	34
$100,000 to $335,000	39
over $335,000	34

A comparison of Tables 4.2 and 4.3 shows that as a result of the Tax Reform Act of 1986, the top corporate tax rate is above the top individual tax rate. Under the corporate form of ownership, any after-tax earnings paid out in the form of dividends to investors will again be taxed at the individual rates. Thus, under the corporate form of ownership, for example, pre-tax earnings of $1 would be subject to a corporate tax rate of 34 percent, thus allowing the firm to earn 66 cents after taxes. If the corporation then chose to pay the 66 cents of net income after taxes to its shareholders in the form of dividends, the distribution would be subject to a 28 percent tax at the individual level, thus leaving the investor with less than 48 cents after taxes (66 cents less 18 cents in personal taxes).

On the other hand if the partnership form of business is chosen, the profits would only be taxed once and at the lower personal rate. Hence, the same dollar of pre-tax profits would yield the investor 72 cents after taxes rather than 48 cents under the corporate alternative. Thus, the corporate form of ownership places a heavy tax burden on its owners.

Role of Marginal Tax Rates

To the extent that income from real estate investments exceeds their expenses, investors are subject to income taxes. Consider various items of the income statement to evaluate the role of marginal taxes on investors' after-tax return, looking first here at rental income, cash expenses, and noncash expenses.

Investors' after-tax return is a function of their marginal tax rates; the following tables use the marginal tax rate to calculate the after-tax cash flow value of pre-tax revenue.

Table 4.4   Income Statement (for the Year Ended 19X1)

Rental income	$18,000
Less:	
Leasing expense	1,800
Maintenance	1,000
Insurance	300
Property taxes	1,200
Interest expense	7,980
Depreciation expense	3,150
Pre-tax profit	$ 2,570

Table 4.5 illustrates the effect of marginal tax rates on the pre-tax profit developed in Table 4.4 based on the individual marginal tax rates of 15 and 28 percent as well as a corporate marginal tax rate of 34 percent.

Table 4.5   After-Tax Profits Based on Varying Marginal Tax Rates

	15%	28%	34%
Pre-tax profit	$2,570	$2,570	$2,570
Tax liability	386	720	874
After-tax profits	$2,184	$1,850	$1,696

As Table 4.5 demonstrates, investors' marginal tax rates play an important role in determining the after-tax cash flow for them associated with a given level of pre-tax profits. An investor in the 15-percent tax bracket receives an after-tax cash flow of $2,184 on pre-tax profits of $2,570, the investor in the 28-percent tax bracket receives only $1,850 after-tax, while the investor in the 34-percent tax bracket (corporate tax rate) after-tax cash flow is only $1,696 on the same pre-tax profit. In all cases, the investors' after-tax cash flow equals the dollar amount of pre-tax profit multiplied by one minus their marginal tax rate (pre-tax profit/[1-MTR]).

Impact of Noncash Expenses

Depreciation represents a noncash expense. Investors have, in the past, been allowed to take these writeoffs against the project revenues even though no cash outlay accompanies these writeoffs and the property will most probably increase in value over time. The value of a dollar of depreciation is directly tied to the taxpayer's marginal tax rate. The higher the marginal rate, the greater the after-tax savings associated with the depreciation deduction.

The structure of the two-bracket tax system (for individual taxpayers) is such that the benefits of depreciation decrease as people are taxed at lower rates. Under the provisions of the Tax Reform Act of 1986, the after-tax value of real estate depreciation is adversely affected due to both lower marginal tax rates and an increase in the required write off period.

Tax Credits under Tax Reform

A tax credit (TC) is a dollar-for-dollar reduction of tax liability. Since a tax credit is used to directly reduce one's tax liability, its worth is independent of the investor's tax bracket. While the Tax Reform Act of 1986 eliminated the regular tax credit for equipment, certain types of real estate may be eligible for tax credits, such as qualified low-income housing, or historic rehabilitation property, for example. The availability of tax credits enhances the investor's after-tax return.

Role of Alternative Minimum Tax

First introduced by Congress as part of the Tax Reform Act of 1968, the alternative minimum tax was designed specifically for those individuals whose tax liabilities had been significantly reduced by the use of so-called tax preference items.

Many of the tax advantages created by Congress were designed to stimulate investment and also, inadvertently or not, allowed many wealthy individuals to escape taxation either partially or completely. This politically unacceptable consequence was the main focus of the Alternative Minimum Tax (AMT). Taxpayers who would otherwise greatly reduce their tax liability through the use of certain tax deductions (tax preferences) are required to recalculate their tax liability using the alternative minimum tax method.

Under this method, taxpayers are required to compute what is called the alternative minimum taxable income (AMTI). This is accomplished by adding the dollar amount of tax preferences to the taxpayer's adjusted gross income and then reducing that total by the amount of alternative tax itemized deductions.

Among the items of tax preference of concern to investors in real estate is excess depreciation. For property placed in service after the signing of the Tax Reform Act of 1986, excess depreciation is defined as the difference between accelerated depreciation (using the present depreciation schedule for 27.5 and 31.5 years) and the amount that would have been written off each year assuming the straight-line method over a 40-year period.

The alternative minimum tax has additional implications for investors who continue to show passive losses from shelter-oriented programs, regardless of when the investment was entered into. Under the Tax Reform Act of 1986, passive losses are an item of tax preference. Hence, investors who were counting on continued deductions due to the phase-in of the passive loss provisions must treat all losses as items of tax preference when calculating the alternative minimum tax.

The alternative minimum taxable income is reduced by the exemption amount to arrive at the excess alternative minimum taxable income. The exemption amount is $40,000 for people filing jointly, $20,000 for married filing separately, and $30,000 for people filing as single taxpayers. The exemption is reduced by 25 percent of the amount that AMTI exceeds $150,000 for joint returns ($75,000 for married filing separate and $112,500 for single filers). The excess alternative minimum taxable income is then taxed at a rate of 21 percent.

In addition to the alternative minimum tax for individual taxpayers, the Tax Reform Act of 1986 enacted an alternative minimum tax for corporate entities; in fact, the corporate alternative minimum tax is much tougher than the individual alternative minimum tax.

At-Risk Rules

Prior to the passage of the "at-risk" rules by Congress in the Tax Reform Act of 1976, many investors were claiming deductions far in excess of their actual dollar economic investment or the amount that they were at risk. Typically, this was achieved through the use of nonrecourse financing that enabled investors to generate losses far greater than they actually stood to lose. In the event that the investment did not pan out, investors stood only to lose their cash investments, since the under nonrecourse financing the lenders could not go after the borrower. Thus, investors were not at risk for the full amount of the investment.

The Tax Reform Act of 1976 sought to eliminate this no-lose situation by limiting the deductibility of investment losses to the taxpayers' economic investment. Thus, under the provisions of the at-risk rules, losses were permitted only to the extent that investors risked personal exposure. However, real property was exempt from the at-risk provisions.

The Tax Reform Act of 1986 extended the at-risk provisions to real property. The new law does not pertain to real property if the investors use "qualified" nonrecourse financing. To be considered qualified nonrecourse debt, the loan must be at market rates and cannot be made by the seller of the property. Thus, nonrecourse financing in most instances still counts in figuring the amount that investors are at-risk.

Investment Interest Limitation

Taxpayers are limited as to the amount of investment interest they can deduct each year. The limit is the dollar amount of their net investment income. Taxpayers are allowed to carry forward indefinitely any unused portion of investment interest, subject to the same yearly limitations.

Summary

Before investing in real estate, investors must consider its economic value as well as its tax implications. An understanding of real estate's sheltering characteristics is essential to any evaluation of its attractiveness in comparison with competing investment choices.

Real estate's ability to provide investors with depreciated deductions and in some instances tax credits enhances its potential after-tax yield. Its ability to reduce taxes is directly related to the taxpayers' marginal tax rates. Along these lines, taxpayers must concern themselves with both the amount and nature of taxable income.

Real estate investors must be concerned not only with the impact of tax rates but also with the character of the property's income and expenses as well. Under the Tax Reform Act of 1986, income is categorized as being active, portfolio, or passive. The tax code places limitations on the use of passive losses to lower tax liability.

In addition to the passive-loss issue, investors must consider the impact of the revised alternative minimum tax, which is intended to require individuals who would otherwise escape taxation through the use of certain tax deductions (tax preferences) to recompute their tax obligations using the Alternative Minimum Tax method. Finally, investors must be aware of the limitations of interest deductibility and the impact of the "at-risk" rules as they pertain to real estate investing.

Chapter 5

Determining the Value of Real Estate Investments

Real estate can provide investors with opportunities to share in the appreciation of property value as well as to benefit from tax savings and cash distributions. Merely purchasing a real estate property does not guarantee appreciation, however. Each real estate investment is unique and therefore must be carefully scrutinized to determine its potential for profitability. Thus, while real estate offers investors the possibility of high returns, it must nevertheless be evaluated on a case-by-case basis. This chapter develops methods of determining a real estate investment's underlying value.

Value Analysis

The evaluation of a real estate investment should begin with a determination of the market value of the property. Investors' potential after-tax return is influenced by the price they pay for the property. If the property is overvalued, appreciation is less likely than if the property is underpriced or priced correctly. Overvaluation results in a lower after-tax return.

Comparable data is available for each type of real estate investment. Investors should compare the asking price with comparable market prices recently paid for similar property to determine whether the price is realistic. While market comparables cannot give a precise value for a piece of property, they can provide a ballpark figure.

Capitalization Rate Approach

An estimate of value can be obtained through use of an overall capitalization rate. This technique involves dividing the property's operating income by a capitalization rate that reflects an investor's required return. Table 5.1 illustrates how the capitalization rate technique works.

Table 5.1 Market Value Comparison—Capitalization Rate Approach

Property	#1	#2
Net operating income	$ 100,000	$ 120,000
Capitalization rate	.10	.10
Market value	$1,000,000	$1,200,000

If a property had a net operating income totaling $100,000 and the capitalization rate were 10 percent, the property would be appraised at $1,000,000 ($100,000/.10). If the property's net operating income were forecast to be $120,000, its value would be $1,200,000.

The capitalization rate varies according to the type of property examined. The capitalization rate is influenced by both the degree of risk associated with the income to be capitalized and by the potential growth in that income. For two investments of equal risk, the one with the greater potential for growth would be capitalized at a lower rate. Risk is the uncertainty surrounding a continuation of the income to be projected. A project whose income stream is more uncertain would be capitalized at a high rate. A project whose income stream is less uncertain would be capitalized at a lower rate.

Rent Multipliers

A valuation method similar to the capitalization rate approach is the use of a gross rent multiplier. This method determines the value of real estate relative to other properties based on a multiple of the property's gross rents. The multiplier can be used to determine whether a given property is properly priced.

Suppose that a property generated $200,000 in gross rents annually and that comparable properties have recently sold at gross rent multipliers of between six to eight. As shown in Table 5.2, this would suggest that the price range should be between $1,200,000 and $1,600,000. This tool enables investors to compare projects on relative terms.

The gross rents multiplier is only a rough indicator of real estate value. For example, a high gross rent multiplier may be justified based on the property's appreciation potential and/or on its attractive tax benefits (historic restorations). A lower gross rent multiplier would be appropriate where the property's costs were higher than those of other similar properties.

Table 5.2 Market Value Estimator—Gross Rent Multiplier

	Low Range	
Property	*A*	*B*
Gross rents earned	$200,000	$400,000
Gross rents multiplier	6	6
Market value	$1,200,000	$2,400,000
	High Range	
Property	*A*	*B*
Gross rents earned	$200,000	$400,000
Gross rents multiplier	8	8
Market value	$1,600,000	$3,200,000

Time Value of Money

Due to high transaction costs, most real estate investments are held for several years. Furthermore, since these investments generate cash flow and tax benefits during the holding phase and significant capital gains when sold, investors must determine not only the actual cash flows but also the timing of the flows. While most investors recognize that there is a time value of money, few incorporate the timing aspect of cash flows into their analyses of investments.

Many tools for measuring the impact of the time value of money on a particular investment opportunity are available to investors. These tools revolve around the concepts embedded in the theory of compounding. An adjustment of cash flows is needed so that investors can compare the value of their cash contributions (outflows) along with the resulting inflows in today's dollars.

Discounted Cash Flow Models

Discounted cash flow techniques compare investment outlays with their forecast cash inflows and tax benefits. These approaches recognize that a dollar received today is more valuable than a dollar received tomorrow, incorporating the time value of money into the decision-making process. Discounted cash flows serve as an exchange-rate mechanism whereby the values of net cash inflows (the excess of cash savings over cash expenditures) realized in the future are adjusted (discounted back) to reflect their present value, thus allowing an "apple-to-apple" basis of comparison. The two most popular discounted cash flow models are net present value and internal rate of return.

Net Present Value The net present value method of analysis involves discounting expected cash flows (cash distributions less tax liability) over the life of the investment at a required rate of return and then comparing the present value of these cash flows with the investment's required outlays.

If the present value of benefits exceeds the present value of required cash outlays, the investment is said to have a positive net present value (that is, present value of the cash in flows minus the present value of the cash outlays), and it would therefore be an investment with a positive return. However, if the investment's present value of cash outlays is greater than the present value of the cash inflows, it would not be acceptable, since the investment fails to achieve investors' minimum required rate of return. Given their required rate of return, investors can then compare alternative investment properties and select those with the highest net present value.

Table 5.3 Net Cash Flows—Real Estate Project

(1) Year	(2) Cash Flow*	(3) Tax Liability	(4) (2) — (3) Net Cash Flow
1	$5,275	$ 720	$4,555
2	5,275	708	4,567
3	5,275	722	4,553
4	5,275	738	4,537
5	5,275	753	4,522
6	5,275	775	4,500
7	5,275	796	4,479
8	5,275	820	4,455
9	5,275	846	4,429
10	25,275	875	24,400
Totals:	$52,750	$7,753	$64,997

*Cash flow includes after tax proceeds from sale of property at the end of year 10.

Example

In the example used throughout Chapter 3, the investor purchased rental property for $100,000, with $20,000 in equity and debt of $80,000 at a rate of ten percent. Table 5.3 reproduces the net cash flows from that hypothetical real estate investment.

Now assume that at the end of ten years, the investor sells the real estate holdings and retires the mortgage. After adjusting for various transaction costs and any taxes due, the net proceeds are $20,000. Comparing the initial outlay of $20,000 with the total net cash flows of $64,997 over the investment's life indicates that the investor's return is well over 200 percent. However, the simple summing of net cash distributions ignores the fact that these cash flows are spread across time and therefore do not reflect the true value of the investment measured in today's dollars.

It is necessary to adjust these amounts to reflect the timing of their occurrence. The net present value approach allows investors to do this. Under the net present value approach, the next step is to apply a discount rate to the yearly net cash distribution column (appearing in Table 5.3) to determine the present value of the investment. The discount rate chosen (12 percent in this example) should correspond to an individual's required rate of return. The investor's required rate of return is determined by calculating what could be earned elsewhere with these funds by the investor.

The present value of the inflows is found by multiplying the net cash distributions column by their corresponding discount factors obtained from Appendix 5.1. Using the 12-percent discount factor, the net cash distributions in Table 5.3 yields the results shown in Table 5.4.

Table 5.4 shows that the present value is $31,957. Since the investor's initial outlay was $20,000, the present value of the inflows is reduced by this amount to establish the net present value of the investment at $11,957.

From the net present value standpoint, the investment would be accepted, since it would provide a return greater than the 12-percent specified. The net present value method does not measure the actual percent rate of return on the investment; it merely determines whether the investment's return is greater or less than the return required.

Internal Rate of Return. The internal rate of return (IRR) model requires the investor to calculate the rate of return of an investment by solving for

Table 5.4   Present Value Analysis—Real Estate Project
(12 Percent Discount Rate)

Year	Net Cash Flow*	Discount Factor	Present Value
1	$4,555	.8929	$4,067
2	4,567	.7972	3,641
3	4,553	.7118	3,241
4	4,537	.6355	2,883
5	4,522	.5674	2,566
6	4,500	.5066	2,280
7	4,479	.4523	2,026
8	4,455	.4039	1,799
9	4,429	.3606	1,597
10	24,400	.3220	7,857
Totals:	$64,997		$31,957

*The $24,000 of net cash flow in year 10 equals $4,400 net cash flow from operations plus $20,000 in net proceeds form the sale of real estate.

the discount factor that causes the present value of the cash flow stream to equal its initial outlay. The formula for calculating the IRR is as follows:

$$PVCI - IO = 0$$

where PVCI represents the present value of cash inflows discounted at the IRR, and IO represents the investment's initial outlay. In the example we have been considering, the IRR is approximately 22.64 percent. This confirms the results of the net present value approach, which indicated that the expected return would be more than the rate of return demanded (12 percent).

Selecting the Discount Rate
The discount rate selected in the net present value approach should represent not only the time value of money, but also the riskiness of the investment itself. For example, an individual who chooses to invest money for a given period of time would want to receive a minimum return in order to maintain the purchasing power he or she had at the time of the original investment. Furthermore, if the investment's return is not certain, the investor would want an additional return to compensate her or him for taking a risk. For this reason, high-risk projects should be discounted at a "hurdle rate" consistent with the expected project risk and the inflation rate forecasted for the invest-

ment period. An additional factor to consider is the potential for inflation. The true value of money lies in the purchasing power. Therefore, to find the true value of an investment, one must adjust the discount rate for anticipated inflation. A higher rate of anticipated inflation requires the use of a higher discount rate.

There is an inverse relationship between the discount rate used and the net present value of an investment, so applying a higher discount rate to a given future cash flow series will cause the present value of the investment to decrease.

Summary

Unlike the situation with many financial assets, whose prices are quoted daily, the evaluation of real estate is often based on its value relative to similar pieces of property. The capitalization rate and the gross rents multiplier are commonly-used approaches to value analysis. These techniques have merits for attaining an initial approximation of an investment's value, but they should only be used to get a ballpark estimate of a property's value.

An accurate evaluation of a real estate investment requires the adjustment of future cash inflows through discounting techniques so that their present worth can be compared with the capital contributions of the investor. Among the various techniques available are net present value and internal rate of return.

Under the net present value method, cash inflows are discounted to reflect the timing of their occurrence and their overall riskiness. The present value of inflows is then compared with the initial outlay to determine if the project provides a minimum acceptable return. If the net present value is positive, the project is minimally acceptable; if the net present value is negative, investors reject it. The discount rate or hurdle rate must reflect not only the impact of inflation but also the risk level of the investment.

The internal rate of return allows investors to calculate the true rate of return on an investment by solving for the discount rate that causes the present value of the inflows to equal the cash outlay. This return is then compared with the investors' desired return to determine the investment's attractiveness. As a practical matter, while calculating the IRR requires the use of a complex mathematical formula, many inexpensive handheld calculators and computerized spreadsheets permit the easy determination of this rate. This form of analysis facilitates the comparison of markedly different investments to determine investors' most desirable course of action.

Chapter 6

Using the Tools of Breakeven Analysis in Real Estate Investing

Chapter 5 demonstrated some techniques for measuring the return on a real estate investment. While measuring the expected return is important, knowing what is needed to break even may be just as important. In an uncertain world, being able to measure the downside risk of an investment is as every bit as important as determining its potential return. Investors must have sensitivity to the assumptions underlying an investment's financial analysis. For example, investors must determine the level of rental income and expenses necessary to ensure a real estate investment's success. This chapter approaches the conditions under which a breakeven point will be reached through an income statement analysis and then through a cash flow analysis, and finally considers the impact of leverage and alternative debt structures on the breakeven point.

Breakeven Analysis

One method of evaluating the rental income capabilities of an real estate investment is breakeven analysis. Under this method, the characteristics of rental income and expenses are examined to identify the investment's breakeven point--the amount of rental income needed to cover all expenses. A comparison of breakeven rental income with forecast rental income levels gives insight into the investment's risks.

The breakeven point is where rental income (RI) equals total costs (TC). Total costs may be broken down into fixed and variable costs. Fixed costs are those that do not vary as rental income varies, although they may vary for other reasons. For example, property taxes do not change as occupancy varies, so property taxes are a fixed cost, even though they may change as a result of a property tax rate change or an assessment change.

61

Variable costs are those that do change as rental income changes. Most operating expenses are fully or partially variable. For example, rental agents receive commissions when they sign tenants to leases. As occupancy increases, rental income and rental commissions increase proportionately. If the lessor provides utilities, an increase in utility expense is attributable to an increase in occupancy and thus to rental income. As a result, utility expenses are a variable cost.

The income statement can be examined to determine what portion of total costs is variable, by using the following formula to evaluate the breakeven point (BEP):

$$BEP = 0 = RI - (TC) = RI - (FC + VC)$$

This equation may be reformulated to read as follows:

$$BEP = FC / ((RI - VC) / RI)$$

The denominator of this formula is often referred to as the marginal contribution because it shows the contribution each dollar of rental income can make to covering fixed cost.

Example

Continuing with the example used in previous chapters, its details are reproduced in Table 6.1. Assume that all costs are fixed except leasing and maintenance expenses, which are expected to equal 15 percent of rental income.

Table 6.1 Income Statement—Real Estate Project

Rental income (revenue)			$18,000
Variable costs:			
Leasing expense	(10%)	$1,800	
Maintenance expense	(5%)	900	
Total variable costs	(15%)	$2,700	
Fixed costs:			
Insurance		400	
Property taxes		1,200	
Depreciation expense		3,150	
Total fixed costs:		$4,750	
Total costs (variable plus fixed costs)			7,450
Pre-tax profit			$10,550

Table 6.1 shows that the variable cost equals $2,700 and fixed costs are projected at $4,750 in the first year. Given the $18,000 rental income figure, the investor can expect $10,550 in pre-tax profit.

To find the breakeven point, an investor merely substitutes the values of fixed cost and variable cost into the breakeven formula:

BEP = FC / ((RI - VC) / RI)

BEP = $4,750 / (($18,000 - $2,700) / $18,000

BEP = $4,750 / (0.85)

BEP = $5,588

According to this analysis, the real estate property must generate rental income of $5,588 in order to break even (to cover both its variable and fixed costs). Every dollar of rental income beyond the breakeven point ($5,588) increases profits by $0.85.

The relationship between rental income, total cost (variable and fixed cost), and the investment's breakeven point is depicted graphically in Figure 6.1. The breakeven rental income level is represented on the graph at the point where the total rental income line intersects the total cost line (variable and fixed costs). At this point, total rental income equals total costs, and therefore total profits would be zero.

The results of breakeven analysis can be verified using an income statement format, as shown in Table 6.2.

Table 6.2   Breakeven Analysis—Income Statement
(for the Year Ended 19X1)

Rental income (revenue)			$5,588
Variable costs:			
Leasing expense	(10%)	$559	
Maintenance expense	(5%)	279	
Total variable costs	(15%)	$838	
Fixed costs:			
Insurance		400	
Property taxes		1,200	
Depreciation expense		3,150	
Total fixed cost:		$4,750	
Total costs (variable plus fixed costs)			5,588
Pre-tax profit			$ 0

Figure 6.1 Breakeven Analysis

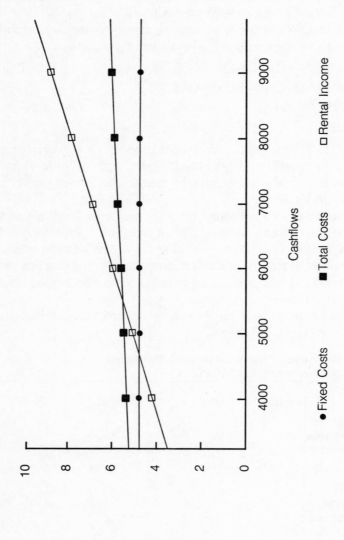

Cashflows

● Fixed Costs   ■ Total Costs   □ Rental Income

BE point = $5588

Table 6.2 shows that the breakeven point is indeed at the point where rental income equals $5,588. The investment will show a loss in the first year as long as total rental income is less than $5,588. If rental income is greater than this amount, the project will show a profit.

Cash Breakeven Analysis

Although the $5,588 of rental income is at the breakeven point, it may still generate a positive cash flow since fixed costs normally include depreciation, which is a noncash expense. We can modify the formula to solve for the cash breakeven point (CBP) by eliminating the dollar amount of depreciation ($3,150) from the fixed costs totals to get cash fixed costs (CFC). The cash breakeven point is calculated as follows:

CBEQ = CFC / ((RI - VC) / RI)

CBEP = $1,600 / (($18,000 - $2,700) / $18,000)

CBEP = $1,600 / (0.85)

CBEP = $1,882

The cash breakeven point is $1,882, as shown in Table 6.3.

**Table 6.3   Breakeven Analysis—Income Statement
(for the Year Ended 19X1)**

Rental income (revenue)			$1,882
Variable costs:			
Leasing expense	(10%)	$188	
Maintenance expense	(5%)	94	
Total variable costs	(15%)	$282	
Fixed costs:			
Insurance		400	
Property taxes		1,200	
Total fixed costs:		$1,600	
Total costs (variable plus fixed costs)			1,882
Pre-tax profit			$ 0

A comparison of the rental income necessary using the standard breakeven point formula and that required using the cash breakeven point formula is quite revealing. The rental income required to cover all cash and noncash expenses is almost three times greater than the rental income necessary to cover the cash expenses.

This comparison indicates that while $5,588 is needed before the investment shows a profit, only $1,882 of rental income is needed before the investor has a positive cash flow. Hence, levels of rental income between the cash breakeven point of $1,882 and the normal breakeven point of $5,588 will provide the investor with a positive cash flow even though the investment will show a loss.

Breakeven Analysis and Leverage

The introduction of financial leverage requires modification of the breakeven formula. In addition to usual operating expenses, the model must carefully consider the impact of interest expense and the repayment of principal. These items represent fixed charges, in the sense that they are not expected to vary with output.

Interest expense, which is a fixed cost, can simply be added to the existing total of fixed costs. While interest expenses are paid from before-tax earnings and are therefore deductible items, the repayment of debt principal must be made from after-tax earnings. This requires an adjustment of the repayment of principal to reflect its pre-tax service requirements.

The leverage breakeven formula enables investors to calculate the level of rental income needed not only to cover fixed operating expenses but also to provide funds for debt servicing requirements. The dollar rental income breakeven point adjusted for leverage can be calculated using the following formula:

$$BEP = (FC + P / (1 - MTR)) / ((RI - VC) / RI)$$

This formula modifies the earlier model by increasing fixed costs by the annual interest charges plus the dollar amount of before-tax funds needed to cover the loan's principal repayment. The total dollars required before tax are related to the amount of the principal payment (P) and the investor's marginal tax rate (MTR).

Example

Remember that the investor borrowed $80,000 to finance the investment over a 30-year period at an interest rate of 10 percent per annum with annual debt servicing requirements of $8,425 ($7,980 in interest expense and $445 in principal repayment the first year). Using this and information provided earlier, the calculation of the initial year's leveraged breakeven point look like this:

$$\text{BEP} = [(FC + (P / (1 - MTR)))] / [(RI - VC) / RI]$$

$$\text{BEP} = \frac{(\$12,730 + (\$445 / (1 - 0.28)))}{(\$18,000 - \$2,700) / \$18,000}$$

$$\text{BEP} = (\$12,730 + \$618) / (0.85)$$

$$\text{BEP} = \$13,348 / (0.85)$$

$$\text{BEP} = \$15,704$$

This analysis reveals that the investment must generate revenues of $15,704 to cover variable costs and fixed costs (including interest charges and required principal repayment). Each dollar of revenue above this level ($15,704) increases profits by $0.85. This relationship is shown graphically in Figure 6.2.

In this example, the use of borrowed funds by the investor increases the breakeven point from $5,588 to $15,704. The use of leverage does in fact increase the riskiness of the investment. The investor originally needed $5,588 in rental income to break even, but the additional fixed cost associated with the use of debt requires a rental income increase of 281 percent to cover all costs. With the potential of additional reward comes the acceptance of additional risk.

As depicted in Figure 6.2, the breakeven point is where the total rental income line intersects the total cost line (variable and fixed costs). In this example, fixed costs include fixed operating expenses, interest expense, and the amount needed before tax to service the yearly principal payment. At this point, total rental income equals total costs, and the total profits (after debt servicing) would be zero.

The breakeven rental income of $15,704 can again be verified using the income statement format. This approach, which incorporates the debt servicing requirements into the analysis, is illustrated in Table 6.4.

Figure 6.2 Breakeven with Leverage

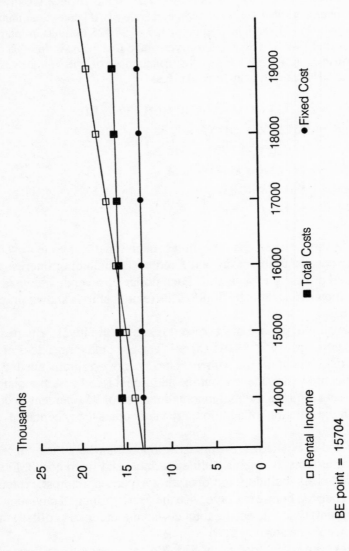

Thousands

BE point = 15704

□ Rental Income   ■ Total Costs   ● Fixed Cost

**Table 6.4   Breakeven Analysis—Leveraged
            (Income Statement for the Year Ended 19X1)**

Rental income (revenue)			$15,704
Variable costs:			
Leasing expense	(10%)	$1,570	
Maintenance expense	(5%)	785	
Total variable costs	(15%)	$2,355	
Fixed costs:			
Insurance		400	
Property taxes		1,200	
Depreciation expense		3,150	
Interest expense		7,980	
Total fixed costs:		$12,730	
Total costs (variable plus fixed costs)			15,085
Pre-tax profit			$ 619
Less:			
Tax liability			$ 174
Funds for principal repayment			$ 445

Table 6.4 confirms that the breakeven point is $15,704. Remember that the investment will still have positive cash flow after debt servicing, since depreciation, a noncash expense, amounts to $3,150 in the initial year. This being the case, it might be interesting to see how much more rental income could drop and still allow the investor to cover all cash flows including the debt servicing requirements.

Cash Breakeven Point and Leverage

As demonstrated in unleveraged example, investors can modify the formula to solve for the cash breakeven point, by subtracting depreciation from our fixed costs. The cash breakeven point then would be calculated as follows:

CBEP =   [CFC + P (1 - MTR)] / [(RI - VC) / RI]

CBEP =   [$9,580 + ($445 / (1 - 0.28)]
$$\frac{}{[\$18,000 - \$2,700] / \$18,000}$$

CBEP =   [$9,580 + $618] / (0.85)

CBEP = $10,199 / (0.85)

CBEP = $11,999

The cash breakeven point (leveraged) or the rental income needed to cover all costs (including debt servicing requirements) is $11,999. The income statement in Table 6.5 verifies that the cash breakeven point is indeed $11,999 in rental income.

Table 6.5　Breakeven Analysis—Leveraged (Income Statement for the Year Ended 19X1)

Rental income (revenue)			$11,999
Variable costs:			
Leasing expense	(10%)	$1,200	
Maintenance expense	(5%)	600	
Total variable costs	(15%)	$1,800	
Fixed costs:			
Insurance		400	
Property taxes		1,200	
Interest expense		7,980	
Total fixed costs:		$9,580	
Total costs (variable plus fixed costs)			11,380
Pre-tax profit			$ 619
Less:			
Tax liability			174
Funds for principal repayment			$ 445

Table 6.5 shows that the breakeven rental income of $11,999 is sufficient to cover all fixed and variable costs while providing the investor with taxable income of $619. Given the investor's marginal tax rate of 28 percent, he or she incurs $172 in taxes (taxable income of $619 times the marginal tax rate of 28 percent) and is left with the $445 necessary to cover the principal repayment requirements.

Summary

This analysis enables the real estate investor to compare forecast rental income with those necessary to break even or cover all costs. A comparison of the two provides insight about the riskiness of an investment. This approach can be adapted to consider leveraged investments in which it is not only necessary to cover operating costs but also debt servicing requirements.

Proper assessment of the desirability of a particular real estate investment can be determined through the use of breakeven analysis, which pinpoints the level of rental income necessary for the investment to break even, in terms of profit generation. This tool can also be adapted to focus on the cash requirements of an investment. Further modifications allow the investor to study the impact of debt financing on the profits and cash requirements of the investment.

Chapter 7

Evaluating Specific Types of Investment

Real estate offers unparalleled opportunity for large investors and small investors alike. Traditional investments are recommended for investors with relatively small capital reserves and investors just entering the real estate area. As long as such investments are made in a prudent manner, with investors taking the time and effort to find and use the necessary information outlined in Chapters 8 through 12, the chances of a successful investment are good.

Aggressive investments, discussed in Chapters 13 through 18, are for investors who have both a shrewd sense of the real estate market and the capital necessary to see a project through to success. The high returns offered by aggressive investments do not come easily or without risk. Individual investors do not have to be wealthy to succeed in aggresive investments; a keen sense of timing, the vision to see value where others do not, an optimistic nature, and tremendous perseverance are far more important factors in achieving investment goals.

Investors who cannot or do not wish to risk the capital necessary to individually finance an aggressive investment can participate in real estate syndication as discussed in Chapter 1 and can use information from Chapters 13 through 18 to evaluate aggressive investment opportunities from that perspective.

Table 7.1, on page 74, provides an overview of ten investment opportunities, as a guide to the relative advantages and disadvantages of the various types of investment opportunities covered in this book.

Profit Potential

The profit potential indicated in Table 7.1 refers to an investment in a prosperous urban area that is experiencing sustained economic growth. In

Table 7.1 Summary of Investment Opportunities

Investment	Profit Potential	Risk	Leverage	Management	Tax Advantages	Liquidity
Traditional						
Single Family	moderate	low	high	high	high	high
Apartment	moderate	low	moderate	low	high	moderate
Condominium	moderate	moderate	high	low	high	moderate
Undeveloped Land	low	high	low	low	low	low
Aggressive						
Mini Storage	moderate	high	moderate	moderate	moderate	moderate
Shopping Center	moderate	high	moderate	high	low	low
Office Bldgs.	high	high	moderate	moderate	moderate	low
Industrial Bldgs.	high	high	moderate	moderate	moderate	low
Mobile Home Parks	high	high	moderate	moderate	low	moderate
Low Income Housing	low	high	moderate	high	high	low

such an area, a project with a high profit potential should earn an IRR (internal rate of return) of between 25 and 40 percent. A similar project with poor profit potential should earn between 8 and 12 percent. This breakdown of categories assumes that investors have the ability to earn 8 percent on their capital without risk (for example, by investing in long-term federal government bonds). When that assumption is true, investors do not want to consider real estate investments with an expected IRR of less than 8 percent.

The advantages and disadvantages of a specific type of investment depend on the individual project under consideration. While some categories of investments are generally preferred over others (depending on an individual investor's needs and circumstances), capital is invested not in general categories, but in particular projects. For example, a poorly located office building coming to market during an office space glut will certainly lose a great deal of money. By contrast, an investment in a particular piece of undeveloped land may unexpectedly blossom overnight and return the investors' money ten-fold.

An analysis of various real estate markets and investor experience with these particular investments strongly suggest consistent variation in returns among different types of investment projects. Developers of office buildings, industrial facilities, and mobile home parks do typically earn an annualized return of 25 to 40 percent. Investors in undeveloped land and low-income housing have generally been much less fortunate. While considerable variation exists from specific project to specific project, investments in single family homes, apartments, condominiums, mini-storage centers, and shopping centers may reasonably expect returns of 15 to 25 percent, based on the experience of other investors.

Risk

With the profit potential of a real estate investment comes proportionally sizeable risk. Even with the greatest possible knowledge of the past and present real estate market, successful real estate investing still requires predicting the future. To forecast accurately the future of a region, a community, a neighborhood, or a particular piece of property, one must know the unknowable. All real estate investments involve an element of risk; some are riskier than others. The guidelines developed in subsequent chapters will help investors identify and evaluate this risk.

In Table 7.1, we assign levels of risk to different investment projects, and we quantify measures of risk to provide a discount rate for the net present value calculation. For the generally least risky investments (single family homes and apartments), we use a discount factor of 12 percent. This represents a 4-percent compensating factor for risk; it is based on the idea that real estate investors, in order to consider any given real estate project, should plan to make at least 4 percent more than they would make in a risk-free alternative. Condominiums are considered moderately risky, so we apply a discounting factor of 15 percent. All other investments are considered high risk, so we apply a 21-percent discount factor in calculating the net present value of those investments. These are average risk factors. Any given real estate project may require a higher or lower factor depending on its individual circumstances.

Leverage

Leverage is the great friend of the real estate investor, helping one dollar do the work of three, four, five, or even ten dollars. The possibility of using leverage is the most attractive factor to the small real estate investor in investing in a single-family house.

We consider highly-leveraged investments to be those where 90 or more percent of the capital employed is financed (e.g., a house in which the investor makes a down payment of 10 percent or less). Moderate leverage is where the capital employed in a real estate project is between 75- and 90-percent financed. Low leverage is anything less than 75-percent financing.

Management

The personal managerial responsibility required of the investor can be negligible or may be critical to the success of a real estate project. Managerial skills are second only to location in determining the success of a shopping center. A successful apartment project requires good management, but the investor can hire such management, making it just another operating expense and freeing the investor from this responsibility.

Table 7.1 ranks the single-family housing investment high in this area, under the assumption that investors generally manage these investments themselves. An apartment building larger than a few units requires professional management unless the investor is willing to undertake this function on a full-time basis, so it is ranked differently in the table. We have ranked low-income housing high because we know of no investors who have ever been able to insulate themselves from management problems in this area.

Tax Advantages

The Tax Reform Act of 1986 generally reduced the tax advantages inherent in real estate. However, it did not eliminate them. For many types of real estate investments, tax considerations make the difference between a positive and a negative return.

The most tax advantages arise from those investments for which the largest portion of the expense is depreciable—i.e., single family units, apartments, and condominiums. The fewest tax advantages are available from investment in undeveloped land. Tax credits generated by restoring old and historic buildings can substantially enhance the desirability of an investment project. (For information about provisions for restoring old and historic buildings, see Chapter 12.)

The enormous tax credits that may be generated by the special treatment for low-income housing in the Tax Reform Act also pose interesting opportunities for investors. This program is so innovative and complex, however, that determination of the net effect of the tax credits on such investments requires sophisticated and extensive examination of each specific case.

Liquidity

Liquidity in real estate is a function of transactions costs and market conditions. Transactions costs vary significantly among the different categories of real estate investments. The general effect of higher transactions costs is to lengthen the holding period necessary to earn a specific rate of return.

The ease with which a real estate property can be converted to cash is often highly dependent on both general monetary and local real estate market conditions. When a scarcity of capital caused interest rates to soar into the high teens in the late 1970s, buyers literally disappeared, and many investors simply found themselves locked into their investment. Conversion under these circumstances resulted in significant losses to many property owners. Local real estate market conditions are also subject to considerable fluctuation from time to time. A particular type of property may be overbuilt, or local economic conditions may deteriorate, making conversion of a property to cash possible only at a distressed price.

Significant differences exist in the liquidity of different types of real estate investments. The most liquid investments in real estate are real estate investment trusts or limited partnerships that are listed on a major exchange. For those investments, numerous participants and low transaction costs result in significant liquidity.

Directly-held real estate is noticeably less liquid. The market for single-family housing is generally very active, but transaction costs may be substantial. The market for condominiums may be as liquid as the single-family market at times, but it is less consistently so. The liquidity of income-producing property (apartments, shopping centers, office buildings, industrial facilities, and mobile home parks) is quite sensitive to both local market and general monetary conditions. High interest rates result in a lower capitalization of the value of an earnings stream and depress the price of such investments. The stability of the income of such a property is of great importance, and locally unsettled market conditions can cast doubt on the reliability of future earnings. Undeveloped land is generally the least liquid of all real estate investments.

All real estate is potentially illiquid. Wise investors always maintain some capital in a liquid form, ready for meeting unexpected needs. Real estate can be a great investment, but it is not the same as money in the bank.

Chapter 8

Single-Family Homes

The simplest form of real estate investment is the single-family home. For many individuals, it is also the best. Investing in single-family homes may provide significant tax advantages, a positive cash flow, and appreciation from a highly-leveraged investment over time. While any investment that offers a high return has risk associated with it, careful investors can control this risk to acceptable levels.

Successful real estate investing is a skill that a person can improve with study and experience over time. Single-family home ownership may be the best way to acquire such experience. Many investors have the rudiments of this knowledge from experience in purchasing their personal residence. Capital requirements are relatively low. Financing arrangements are standardized. The market is the most liquid in this type of real estate. Ample knowledge about property availability and location, market conditions, and future trends are readily available. The investor would normally be the sole owner of the property giving her or him maximum control and flexibility. The management of the property is relatively simple.

Investing in a single-family home requires a different perspective from purchasing a home for residential purposes. To be successful as an investor, one must analyze each potential investment's likely financial performance and evaluate whether it is worth the time, trouble, and risk. The preferred way to analyze the investment is by calculating its internal rate of return (see Chapter 3) because this encompasses the effect of all cash flows over time.

The critical factors affecting the financial performance of the investment are its price, the cost of financing, the rental potential of the property, and the potential appreciation of the property.

Price

The best price is not necessarily the lowest price. Price is but one of four components that affect return. An excessively low price is not a good deal if the location of the property means it will be difficult to rent at a level generating a positive cash flow. A 20-percent differential in the price of a house can often mean the difference between a neighborhood that is deteriorating and a neighborhood that is growing. Paying 25 percent above the market value for a house where the seller is willing to finance the property at interest levels well below the market can be a great deal. Successful investors take into consideration all factors that affect the total rate of return.

Of course, other things being equal, it is always preferable to purchase at a lower price. Prior to making a commitment, investors should thoroughly shop the market they are interested in and develop the ability to spot value. This task is made much easier by the abundance of real estate agents who will be glad to assist investors' in their search. While there is always the chance of an exception, the general rule is that houses selling below their true value are as common as hen's teeth. This does not mean investors cannot find properties that will yield a handsome profit. It means that most residential real estate markets are relatively efficient and most homes sell at the market price.

Profit for investors lies in their ability to recognize value in a property not yet recognized by the market. Most single-family homes are purchased for residential purposes, and the focus is on the amenities relative to the needs of the purchaser. Investors must consider the discounted value of the cash flows that a single-family dwelling may consume or produce in evaluating the desirability of a particular piece of property.

Foreclosures, Tax Sales, and Probate Sales

Many investors have found that substantial profits can be obtained in the housing market by purchasing property in foreclosure, property in probate, or property at tax sales and auctions for less than their market value. The underlying notion behind such a strategy is that as a result of circumstances, sellers are not able to obtain full value of the property. As a result of the success of those who first used this strategy and its subsequent popularity, there is now great competition for such properties. Finding, and completing, a successful investment in these properties requires a great deal of time and effort. In addition, this approach to real estate investment contains many pitfalls to trap the inexperienced investor.

Property in foreclosure often has no equity left in it. Where there is equity, the owners, however distressed, may be well aware of such equity. Property purchased in this manner is generally "as is" with no recourse to the seller. Probate sales are generally court-supervised to ensure that the estate receives fair market value for the property being disposed of. Tax sales and auctions are frequently quite competitive where the property has desirable investment characteristics. The title to a property obtained through a tax sale may be clouded and difficult to obtain a mortgage on. In addition, purchasing a property at tax sales or auctions does not provide investors with opportunities for contingencies that give normal purchase contracts needed flexibility.

It is possible to uncover a gem in foreclosure, probate, tax or auction sales, but the likelihood of doing so is remote. Seeking profit in this manner is more like to prospecting than investing.

Financing

Investors have many options in financing a single-family residence. Investors may seek conventional financing, assume the seller's mortgage, or utilize seller financing. The conventional fixed-rate mortgage characterized by an unchanging rate of interest and an unchanging total interest and principle payment over a specified period of time remains popular with buyers.

Where the investor assumes the seller's mortgage and combines this with another mortgage, the financing package is referred to as a wraparound. This would be done where the seller's mortgage is assumable and has a lower rate than the current market.

An astounding array of new types of mortgages have recently been made available from conventional sources. As a result of the general decline in interest rates in the mid 1980s and a rush to refinance by those who had obtained mortgages at higher interest rates, many banks now offer convertible fixed-rate mortgages (at a higher interest rate) where the mortgagee has a one-time option to elect a lower prevailing rate of interest.

Adjustable-rate mortgages, where the rate of interest applied to the principle varies according to changes in the general rate of interest, also became common in the past decade. The advantage of an adjustable-rate mortgage lies in its lower rate of interest relative to a fixed-rate mortgages. However, an upward change may substantially increase the payments on a property.

An adjustable-rate mortgage may or may not have a cap on its interest rate. A cap is generally a maximum limit to which the interest rate can rise; another kind of cap controls the level of payments. When the payments are capped but the interest rate is not, the possibility of negative amortization arises. Negative amortization occurs when the payment is less than the interest charged and the difference is added to the mortgage balance.

FHA 203 fixed-rate mortgages are designed to have negative amortization in the early years of the mortgage to give purchasers the lowest possible initial mortgage payments. Some adjustable-rate mortgages can be converted to fixed-rate mortgages at the option of the mortgagee.

Successful investors give careful consideration to the form of the mortgage, considering the tradeoffs between the usual option of higher points up front or a higher rate of interest on the duration of the mortgage. (See Chapter 2 for more information.) The effect of these considerations on total return can be explored through the use of the internal rate of return or net present value models. (See Chapter 5 for more information.)

Evaluating Rental Potential

The desirability of a given property depends on how well it meets the needs of those who would be willing to rent it. To evaluate the relative desirability of a specific property, it helps to think in terms of market segments. Market segments occur because different types of renters have distinctive housing preferences. Significant market segments include singles, young couples with no children, young couples with young children, divorcees with children, established families, empty nesters, and active retirees. Each group has different needs and concerns relative to location (nearness to work and shopping), public amenities (schools, libraries, public transportation, parks), social amenities (churches, neighborhood composition), and building characteristics (layout, yard, bedrooms, kitchens, storage).

The determination of how rentable a property is should be undertaken on the basis of how well the property meets the needs of the relevant market segment or segments. The variables to focus on are the current level of rents and rental vacancies for comparable properties and what will happen to these variables in the future.

Potential Appreciation

An important advantage of investing in a single-family residence is the opportunity to sell it as either a personal residence or an income-producing property. This allows investors to maximize the potential for appreciation in their investment. The potential for appreciation in either of these markets depends on many factors. While the national trend in single-family housing prices has consistently risen since World War II, the rate of increase has been uneven, and considerable variation takes place between and within regions.

Some of these factors the potential investor cannot control or escape. Escalating interest rates and monetary shortages put pressure on housing prices. Shifts in industry conditions (the petroleum industry in Texas, the automotive industry in the Midwest) or shifts in the desirability of different regions (the impact of the oil shortage of the Northeast relative to the Sunbelt) may also adversely affect prices.

The investor can control some factors that affect the potential for appreciation by selecting an appropriate property. One set of factors has to do with building characteristics: structural soundness, neighborhood setting, style, and size are important considerations. A second, perhaps more important, set of factors involve the location of the property: the stability of the community, emerging patterns of commercial and industrial development, and the future location of public amenities all affect the desirability of a particular location.

General Investment Characteristics

Strengths

Profit Potential. The return on this form of investment may be significantly higher than for other types of investments. The attractiveness of the investment lies in the presence of some tax sheltering effect, the prospect of a positive cash flow, and the potential for appreciation. Through the careful selection of appropriate properties, investors may substantially enhance their personal wealth.

Ease of Financing. The relatively low price of this type of investment, combined with the availability of a large and diverse mortgage industry, increases the attractiveness of single-family housing to investors with little capital. In addition, the investment may be highly leveraged. Financing of up to 80 percent is available with conventional mortgages and 95% with MGIC (Mortgage Guarantee Insurance Corporation) mortgage insurance. Even greater leverage is possible through a variety of governmental programs (primarily VA and FHA). The mortgage may be secured by some combination of the borrower's ability to pay and the value of the property itself.

Liquidity. The market for single-family housing is generally quite liquid. At any time, numerous residences are offered for sale, and numerous buyers are looking for homes. This means investors can shop at their leisure until they find property that precisely meets their needs. When the time comes to sell, the presence of numerous buyers assure that investors can receive a fair market value for the property.

Control. Since this type of investment requires relatively little capital, an investor of limited means can be the sole owner of the property. The ability to fully control all aspects of an investments' profitability is not a small advantage. If the investor has a partner, he or she would need to reach an agreement about property management policies, rent levels, the timing and conditions of the sale, etc. If the investor were a limited partner in a syndicate, he or she would have no voice in these decisions at all. The ability to control the fate of one's investment in accordance with one's needs is very important to many potential investors.

Weaknesses

Loss of Rental Income. Loss of rental income is an important risk in single-family residences, since the cash flow is then zero while expenses continue. Loss of rental income can be expected between the time one tenant leaves and a new tenant is found. This loss may be controlled by having a well-drawn lease that requires proper notification of intent to leave. A danger occurs if the market weakens to the point that it takes a significant period of time to find a new tenant and/or the rent level must be reduced to attract a new tenant.

Loss of rental income can occur when a tenant can't or won't pay rent. If the tenant refuses to leave, an eviction process must be started which can be both expensive and time-consuming. Loss from this source can be minimized through careful tenant selection policies.

Potential Change in Tax Laws. The possibility always exists that the government will change the tax laws to reduce the net return on a property, thus decreasing its value.

Rent Controls. Rent control is a specter that haunts real estate investors. The argument that rent controls make little economic sense often crumbles in the face of a politician willing to cater to a misinformed public. Urban areas appear particularly vulnerable to this circumstance.

Management Costs. Investors frequently personally manage their single-family home property. This reduces expenses and places greater control in the hands of the investor.

A critical element of property management is the selection of good tenants. What makes tenants "good" is that they pay the rent on time and take care of the property. Therefore, in selecting tenants, investors should check credit references of prospective tenants and consult the management of their last place of residence. In this day of consumer rights, getting rid of undesirable tenants can be a time consuming and expensive process. Selecting good tenants eliminates this problem.

Firms that specialize in property management are available for single-family property investors, but frequently most such companies prefer to manage multi-unit dwellings. Sometimes, a local real estate agency or agent can be found to provide this service at a reasonable cost.

Tax Considerations

The tax shelter available from a single-family investment property has been diminished by the Tax Reform Act of 1986 (TRA) but remains a significant factor for many individuals. As explained in Chapter 2, single-family residences can be depreciated over 27.5 years. This creates a noncash expense that the investor can use to shield income and/or capture tax savings.

Tax savings arise when a property produces a loss that can be applied against earned income adjustable gross income. The possible reduction of earned income is limited to $25,000. Tax savings under the current law could therefore be as high as $7,500 per year for an individual in the 28-percent bracket or $8,333 for an individual subject to the 5-percent surcharge. In addition, property losses may be used to offset other passive income without limit.

The elimination of the capital-gains tax by the TRA means that an investor's net gain on the sale of a property is taxed at the same rate as ordinary income. For investors filing joint tax returns, this means a rate of 15 percent up to $32,450, then 28 percent up to $78,400, then a rate of 33 percent up to $185,000, and 28 percent thereafter. The gain to be taxed is the difference between the net selling price and the basis (the cost of the property less depreciation expense).

Case Study

Acquisition Stage. Since single-family rental property can be owned individually due to its affordability, this case study involves an investment held outright by the investor.

Table 8.1 presents a schedule of the initial sources and uses of funds for the hyphothetical investment. Total funds required are $106,000. The rental property cost is $100,000, and settlement costs (including mortgage points) are estimated to be $6,000.

Table 8.1 Single-Family Home Investment Data

Capital required:

Cost of property (land at $15,000)	$100,000
Points (2%)	1,600
Additional closing costs	3,400
Total capital required:	$106,000

Sources of capital:

Mortgage (10% for 20 years)	$ 80,000
Investor's capital	26,000
Total capital provided:	$106,000

Holding Stage. The investor secures a mortgage for $80,000 (80 percent of the appraised value of the property) at an annual rate of 10 percent. The mortgage amortization period is 20 years. The investor supplies the remaining $26,000.

Table 8.2 presents the mortgage amortization schedule for the loan, showing the $9,264 annual debt servicing requirement.

Table 8.3 on page 92 presents an income statement for the project. Gross rental income is forecast to increase by six percen per year. Total operating costs are estimated at $1,975 and are forecast to increase by three percent per year. Additionally, the investor has annual interest and depreciation as additional expenses.

The investment results in a $600 loss in year one. Since the investor's adjusted gross income is less than $100,000, placing her or him in the 28-percent tax bracket, the tax savings from the investment is $168 (which is 28 percent of $600).

Table 8.2 Loan Amortization Schedule $80,000 20-Year Loan (10 percent)

Year	Total Interest	Principal Payment	Total Payment	Remaining Balance
1	$7,940.43	$1,323,81	$9,264.24	$78,676.20
2	7,801.80	1,462.44	9,264.24	77,213.77
3	7,648.67	1,615.57	9,264.24	75,598.20
4	7,479.50	1,784.74	9,264.24	73,813.47
5	7,292.60	1,971.64	9,264.24	71,841.84
6	7,086.13	2,178.11	9,264.24	69,663.72
7	6,858.08	2,406.16	9,264.24	67,257.55
8	6,606.13	2,658.11	9,264.24	64,599.44
9	6,327.79	2,936.45	9,264.24	61,662.99
10	6,020.30	3,243.94	9,264.24	58,419.05
11	5,680.63	3,583.61	9,264.24	54,835.44
12	5,305.37	3,958.87	9,264.24	50,876.57
13	4,890.81	4,373.43	9,264.24	46,503.14
14	4,432.87	4,831.37	9,264.24	41,671.77
15	3,926.97	5,337.27	9,264.24	36,334.49
16	3,368.08	5,896.16	9,264.24	30,438.33
17	2,750.67	6,513.57	9,264.24	23,924.77
18	2,068.59	7,195.65	9,264.24	16,729.11
19	1,315.12	7,949.12	9,264.24	8,779.99
20	482.76	8,779.99	9,264.24	0

The investment earns a profit within two years and generates taxable income in years three through ten as a result of the dollar amoung of rental income increasing faster than the dollar amount of expenses. In fact, interest expense decreases over the holding period as the loan is paid down.

While the income statement provides the investor with information regarding the tax effect of the hypothetical investment it does not present a complete picture of his financial status. In order to see how the investor fares in year one it is also necessary to determine the cash flow resulting from the investment.

Thus, the next step in our analysis is the determination of the amount of yearly net cash flows associated with the hypothetical investment. Table 8.4 on page 93 depicts the annual cash flow statement for the investment over the 10-year investment horizon. It is interesting to note that in our example the cash flow improves over time, since the debt servicing requirements (by

Table 8.3 Income Statement Real Estate Project

Year	1	2	3	4	5
Rental Income	$12,000	$12,720	$13,483	$14,292	$15,150
Operating Ex					
Main	600	636	674	715	757
Insur	105	111	118	125	133
Prop	900	954	1,011	1,072	1,136
Depr	2,975	3,060	3,060	3,060	3,060
Interest	8,020	7,882	7,729	7,560	7,373
Profit (loss)	($600)	$77	$891	$1,761	$2,690
Tax Effect	$168	($21)	($249)	($493)	($753)

Year	6	7	8	9	10
Rental Income	$16,059	$17,022	$18,044	$19,126	$20,274
Operating Ex					
Main	803	851	902	956	1,014
Insur	141	149	158	167	177
Prop	1,204	1,277	1,353	1,434	1,521
Depr	3,060	3,060	3,060	3,060	3,060
Interest	7,166	6,938	6,686	6,408	6,100
Profit (loss)	$3,685	$4,748	$5,884	$7,100	$8,402
Tax Effect	($1,032)	($1,329)	($1,648)	($1,988)	($2,353)

far the largest cash outflow) are fixed while rental income increase 6 percent and operating expenses increase by 3 percent per annum.

Disposal Stage. The property appreciates at six percent per year over the 10-year holding period and has closing costs of six percent. To determine the tax liability and resulting after-tax cash flow, however, the investor must determine the property's basis (the initial price plus nonexpensed closing costs less the sum of annual depreciation expenses over the holding period).

Table 8.4 Cash Flow Statement Real Estate Project

Year	1	2	3	4	5
Rental Income	$12,000	$12,720	$13,483	$14,292	$15,150
Operating Ex					
Main	600	636	674	715	757
Insur	105	111	118	125	133
Prop	900	954	1,011	1,072	1,136
Debt	9,264	9,264	9,264	9,264	9,264
Cash flow	$1,131	$1,755	$2,416	$3,117	$3,859

Year	6	7	8	9	10
Rental Income	$16,059	$17,022	$18,044	$19,126	$20,274
Operating Ex					
Main	803	851	902	956	1,014
Insur	141	149	158	167	177
Prop	1,204	1,277	1,353	1,434	1,521
Debt	9,264	9,264	9,264	9,264	9,264
Cash flow	$4,647	$5,482	$6,366	$7,304	$8,298

Table 8.5 Basis Calculation

Acquisition costs	$100,000
Plus:	
Closing costs	6,000
	$106,000
Less:	
Accumulated depreciation	30,515
Points written off	800
Adjusted basis	$ 74,685

Table 8.6 shows the computation of the investor's tax liability at the time the property is sold, by first subtracting the adjusted basis ($74,685) from the net (i.e., gross sale price less closing costs) to arrive at taxable income of

Table 8.6 Tax Liability

Net sale price	$168,335
Less:	
Adjusted basis	74,685
Gain on sale	$ 93,650
Tax liability (at 28%)	$ 26,222

$93,650. This amount is then subject to the investor's tax rate of 28 percent, for a tax liability of $26,222.

Having established the tax liability, the investor finds the after-tax cash flow by subtracting the sum of closing costs, mortgage balance ($58,419; see Table 8.2), and taxes from the gross sale price of $179,080. The after-tax cash flow at the disposal stage is $83,694 (see Table 8.7).

Table 8.7 After-Tax Cash Flow

Selling price	$179,080
Less:	
Selling expenses	$10,745
Mortgage	58,419
Tax	26,222
After-tax cash flow	$ 83,694

The after-tax rate of return is composed of three components: the project's cash flow during the investment phase; the tax effects over the holding phase; and the after-tax reversion. Table 8.8 present these components for the case study. The after-tax rate of return (IRR) on the $26,000 of invested capital is 20.2 percent, and the investment's net present value at 12 percent is $20,100.

Table 8.8 Summary of Investor Return

Year	Sum Invested	Tax Benefits (Liability)	Cash Flows	Due to Reversion	Yearly Amounts
0	($26,000)				$(26,000)
1		$ 168	$ 1,131		1,299
2		(21)	1,755		1,734
3		(249)	2,416		2,167
4		(493)	3,117		2,624
5		(753)	3,859		3,106
6		(1,032)	4,647		3,615
7		(1,329)	5,482		4,153
8		(1,648)	6,366		4,718
9		(1,988)	7,304		5,316
10		(2,353)	8,298	$83,694	89,639
Total		($9,698)	$44,375	$83,694	$92,371

IRR = 19.4%
NPV = $17,909

Summary

Single-family housing is one of the most desirable real estate investments, particularly for small or inexperienced real estate investors. The potential gains from this investment are substantial and enhanced by the current tax law. Investors have control, a relatively high degree of liquidity, and access to readily-available financing. These advantages compare favorably for many investors with the disadvantages of personally managing the property and potential rent controls or changes in the tax law.

The key factor in a successful single-family investment property is its location. A desirable location helps ensure good tenants and appreciation in the value of the property. Investor must carefully examine the relevant housing market to determine the appropriate price to pay for the property, the most desirable form of financing, and the cash flow that can be realistically expected over the anticipated investment period. Considering these attributes of the property from the perspective of discounted cash flows helps successful investors make wise choices.

Chapter 9

Apartments

The end of the 1980s and the beginning of the 1990s present great opportunities for careful investors to invest in apartments in almost all regions of the United States. A number of powerful forces combine to create this effect.

Supply

On the supply side, the Tax Reform Act of 1986 significantly reduced taxpayers' incentive to develop sizeable apartment projects by extending the depreciation period and limiting the amount of passive loss that can be used to offset earned income. While this type of investment still provides exciting opportunities for small investors as individuals or acting through a syndication such as a limited partnership, the market adjustment will be slow to adapt to the new environment. One reason for this is that many large investors feel "burned" by the change in the rules of the game.

Demand

The demand for multiple-family units in general may also be expected to rise strongly during this period. This increase in demand will come from three sources: changing lifestyles, changing demographics, and the continuing rise in the price of single-family housing.

As a society we appear to be moving to generally less-committed lifestyles. Inter- and intra- regional mobility has been on the increase since World War II and may be expected to increase in the future. Family situations are less stable. The divorce rate appears to have stabilized at 50 percent for first marriages, but "living in" relationships are increasingly common. Young people are delaying family formation either to develop their careers or because of a general cynicism about family stability. People often mirror the uncertainty in their personal lives in their choice of residence. This implies a reduced frequency of home ownership and greater demand for apartment housing.

The underlying demographics also favor the shift from owning a house to renting an apartment. In the late 1980s and the 1990s, baby boomers are approaching or passing through their forties. Increasingly, they are becoming empty nesters who may no longer need or desire a single family residence. Advances in medical science have contributed to longevity and created a healthier and more active elderly population.

Many older people prefer apartment living because of the absence of maintenance and ownership responsibilities. Apartment room layouts also tends to favor their lifestyle. The lower income associated with retirement years and the Tax Reform Act combine to reduce the tax incentive for home ownership among the elderly.

The continued rise in the price of single-family housing may also increase the demand for apartment residences. The average new single-family residence now sells for over $100,000. Home ownership rates increased slightly during the 1960s and 1970s because of the emergence of the predominate two-earner family. Both spouses in a family working increased family purchasing power and enabled families to purchase a home despite escalating costs. However, labor force participation rates of women appear to have peaked. Without additional family workers, for many families the increase in family income will not be sufficient to catch spiraling housing costs.

Housing costs rise because of increased land prices and increased construction costs. It is difficult to see a reduction in the future rate of increase of either of these costs. Consequently, families will choose apartments at an increasing rate. Of course these forces will not necessarily influence properties in all parts of the country similarly. Significant differences in regional rates of growth will magnify or diminish these effects. Even within a given community, some properties will surely fall in value as others appreciate. Location remains the key to value for any type of residential property.

Determining Value in Apartment Buildings

Good Deals and Bad Deals

Unlike single-family homes in which amenity attributes are an important determinant of value, the value of apartments is determined by their ability to earn a return for the investor. Knowledgeable investors develop the ability to see value in a property unrecognized by others. How good a deal is depends on a combination of price, financing terms, rentability, expenses, and the potential for appreciation. The discounted cash flow approach may be used to reconcile these different factors. A well-located, well-maintained property that can be acquired with little capital and an immediate positive cash flow would certainly be attractive. Equally attractive might be a poorly-maintained property that currently has a negative cash flow but has the potential to be turned around with some upgrading and proper management.

Each investment opportunity must be evaluated on its own terms. Successful investors do not focus on one or two facets of the investment. They evaluate the property as a whole. In today's market, the most frequently encountered opportunity is a multifamily property that initially has a negative cash flow but has good potential to be upgraded and to yield a positive cash flow with better management. The financial returns on such an investment can be spectacular.

Types of Apartments

Apartment units may be contained in garden-level buildings or high-rises. Garden-level apartment buildings have up to three levels. High-rises have more than three levels. High-rises are differentiated from garden apartments by substantially higher construction costs having to do with structural requirements and elevators. High-rise apartments are generally constructed where the population is dense, so the cost of land is frequently higher as well. High-rises also tend to serve market segments where location and amenities are more important factors than price in determining occupancy rates.

Garden apartments may be designed as flats (one floor) or townhouses (two or more floors). Units may have individual or shared entrances. Utilities may be provided by the landlord or be the responsibility of individual tenants. Garden apartments frequently have amenities such as a pool, play areas, and open spaces.

Demand for Rental Units

The factors that affect the demand for apartment units are based on the ability of a given property to meet the needs of those who would be willing to rent it. To evaluate a specific property in this way, it helps to think in terms of market segments. Market segments occur because different types of renters have distinctive housing preferences. Relevant market segments include singles, young couples without children, young couples with young children, divorcees with children, established families, empty nesters, active retirees.

Many successful apartments cater to mixed market segments. However, there appears to be a trend toward orienting a project to particular market segments on the theory that individuals in similar circumstances have a natural propensity to group together.

Each group has different needs and concerns relative to location (nearness to work and shopping), public amenities (schools, libraries, public transportation, parks), social amenities (churches, neighborhood composition), and building characteristics (layout, yard, bedrooms, kitchens, storage).

The determination of how rentable a given property is should be undertaken on the basis of how well the property meets the needs of the relevant market segment or segments. The variables to focus on are the current level of rents and rental vacancies for comparable properties and what will happen to these variables in the future.

GRM and CPU

A first approximation of how valuable an apartment property is can be gained by determining its gross rent multiple (GRM). The GRM is calculated by dividing the potential gross rents, assuming each unit is occupied, into the price of the building. Real estate agents are well versed in expressing the value of an apartment property in terms of its GRM. The prevailing GRM varies from region to region and within a given area for individual types of properties because of differences in maintenance costs, rental vacancies, potential for rent increase, potential for appreciation, and general market conditions. In many areas, GRMs range from 6 to 12 with 8 being considered worth an investor's further investigation.

Cost per unit (CPU) divides the total number of units into the price of an apartment property. An apartment building with a $35,000 CPU is not necessarily a better investment than an apartment with a $40,000 CPU. Many factors influence total return. CPU is a shorthand method of expressing value—given many other important factors.

Potential Appreciation

The potential for appreciation in a multifamily property depends on its earning power. Given current market supply and demand factors, investors may expect that a well-maintained property in a desirable location will have its rents rise at least as rapidly as the general level of prices.

Investing in an apartment building with low occupancy rates that can be cured by upgrading the property is another means of increasing earning power, which in turn increases the value of the property when future buyers capitalize the earnings stream in order to determine its value.

An important advantage associated with an investment in apartment properties is their relative ability to stand inflationary pressures. As long as the demand for rental units remains fairly strong, rents can be raised to off-set increasing expenses. Turbulent economic conditions often actually have the effect of increasing the demand for rental units.

Some factors that effect the potential for appreciation are controlled by a property location that is desirable from the point of view of potential tenants. The stability of the community, emerging patterns of commercial and industrial development, and the future location of public amenities all affect the changing desirability of a particular location.

Another set of factors have to do with the characteristics of the specific property. The structural soundness of the building, the condition of the roof, plumbing, and heating and cooling systems all contribute to the total return on the property.

Analyzing the Fact Sheet

When an apartment is placed on the market, the owner develops what is referred to as a "fact sheet"—sometimes called a setup sheet. This will (or should) detail the rental rolls, the types of leases current tenants hold, current and available financing, and an array of costs associated with building maintenance and operations. This information should be treated as a starting point for your own analysis.

A situation investors frequently encounter is one in which, in order to maximize profits or conserve cash, the present apartment owner has deferred maintenance and cheapened operations to the point where the operation has high vacancy rates, high turnover, and low rents (because of the relative lack of desirability of the rental units). This is not a bad situation. For the smart investor, it spells o–p–p–o–r–t–u–n–i–t–y.

Preparing to Make an Offer

Through speaking with other landlords, bankers, and property management professionals, the investor should develop an accurate estimate of how much expenses would actually run for the property. These include reserves for vacancies, lost rent, insurance, landscaping and snow removal, common area maintenance (including swimming pools), overall building repair, new tenant preparation expenses, replacement costs for appliances and carpet, and professional management fees.

An investor should also assess current rent levels. Are they competitive? Too low a turnover rate and too few vacancies may mean rents are too low. What might a future rent structure be, and how long would it take to get there? With this knowledge, an investor is properly equipped to evaluate the terms of an offer for the property.

General Investment Characteristics

Strengths

High Potential Profit Levels. The 1990s will be characterized by an increasing demand for apartments. Given present supply limitations, a general rise in rental housing costs may be expected. This will have the effect of increasing the cash flow and profitability. As these income levels are capitalized into price, the potential for long-term appreciation in the value of rental income properties is seen.

Leverage. Where a stable track record of financial performance may be demonstrated, bankers find investment in apartments to be desirable. Conventional equity financing is often available for 75 to 80 percent of the property's value. A variety of mortgage contracts are available, as they are for single-family residences.

An additional source of capital commonly used in apartment property is a second mortgage from the seller. Depending on the circumstances and the buyer's negotiating skills, use of this source of financing can significantly increase a property's attractiveness.

Reduced Rent Risk. As rents are received from a number of independent individuals, the failure of one tenant to pay does not reduce cash flow to zero.

Liquidity. In most markets an active group of buyers is always searching for good multifamily residential properties. Turnaround times for a seller are often comparable to those existing in the single-family housing market.

Weaknesses

Size. Many apartment properties are too large for a single individual to undertake. A single investor may join a syndicate to purchase a larger property. The syndicate may take the form of a simple partnership, corporation, limited partnership, or master limited partnership. (The advantages and disadvantages of the different real estate ownership forms are discussed in Chapter 1.) Any form of joint ownership will reduce the investor's control over the investment.

Management. Where the investor is a general partner or owns the property outright, he or she has considerable management responsibility. To some extent, this responsibility can be limited by the employment of property management professionals or a tenant who provides services for a rent reduction. In either case, the investor retains ultimate responsibility for the success of the investment. Experience in this area suggests that the involvement of the investor in managerial matters will be greater than anticipated.

Rent Control. The threat of rent control is significant. Local politicians tend to respond to demands of tenants who are squeezed by market forces, regardless of how negative the consequences of rent control may be in the long run. Given anticipated trends in the supply of, and demand for, rental units, this threat may increase in the future.

One of the most attractive features of investing in rental property is the ability to pass costs through to the tenants. Rent control strikes at the heart of this relationship. Since multifamily rental property is valuable only to the extent that it produces a return on the investment, rent control directly affects the value of such property.

Potential Change in Tax Laws. The Tax Reform Act of 1986 placed at a disadvantage those investors who had committed capital to multifamily housing prior to 1987 under a different set of rules. Tax law may be changed to favor or discourage this type of investment. A cautious investor would be wise to structure an investment in rental property in such a way that it would be profitable with or without the current treatment of this type of income under the present tax code.

Tax Considerations

As with other real estate investments, depreciation expenses on an apartment building may be used to shield a limited amount of income from taxes. Residential property can be depreciated over a 27.5-year period on a straight-line basis. Losses may be carried over to apply against earned income up to

$25,000 if the investor materially participates in the management of the property. This income offset may yield an individual a maximum tax saving of $8,333 depending on tax bracket. Losses from actively-managed investment property may be fully applied against other passive income.

If an investor participates in a limited partnership in residential properties, the limited partners' share of losses do not have to be proportionate with their share of cash distributions. This means that an investor could receive 10-percent losses (to apply against other passive income) and 5-percent of the cash distribution. This attribute of the limited partnership ownership form enhances its desirability relative to other business forms as a vehicle for the small investor in large apartment rental properties.

Case Study

Acquisition Stage. Larger real estate investments are often structured as syndications. Under current tax law, newly-generated passive losses can only be used to offset passive income, as a result many real estate investments are being structured as unleveraged limited partnerships. These limited partnerships generate passive income that can be used in conjunction with passive losses to provide investors with higher after-tax returns.

The tax treatment of limited partnerships is much more complicated than that for individuals and corporations. In order to demonstrate these concepts within the framework of a real estate syndication, this case study involves an investment in an apartment building limited partnership, with details provided in Table 9.1.

Holding Stage. Table 9.2 presents the partnership's forecast profit (loss) statements from years one through ten based on the information in the table and assumptions (given below) about underlying the forecast profit-and-loss statements.

Revenue is forecast at $720,000 in year one and expected to increase six percent per year. Organizational expenses of $118,000 are amortized over the first five years at an annual rate of $23,600. Operating expenses represent 15 percent (including leasing expense) of rental income. The partnership's profit represents rental income less the sum of organizational, operating, and depreciation expenses. The partnership's tax liability total tax liability can be calculated by multiplying the yearly profits by 28 percent. The limited partners' tax liability equals 99 percent of the total tax liability.

Table 9.1 Apartment Complex Limited Partnership Assumptions

Number of units offered	200
Total equity raised	$6,650,000
Equity contribution per limited partnership unit	33,250
Cost of apartment units	5,400,000
Land costs	600,000
Securities commissions (8 percent)	532,000
Organizational expenses (amortized over 60 months)	118,000
Assumed value (end of year 10)	13,500,000
Selling expenses	3%
Operating expenses (as percentage of revenue)	15%
Limited partners' tax bracket	28%
Limited partners' share of profit (losses)	99%
General partners' share of profits (losses)	1%
Limited partners' share of cash distributions	99%
General partners' share of cash distributions	1%
Limited partners' share of residual cash flow	99%
General partners' share of residual cash flow	1%

Table 9.2 Apartment Complex Profit (Loss) Statement—28-Percent Tax Bracket

Year	1	2	3	4	5
Rental income	$720,000	$763,200	$808,992	$857,532	$908,983
Less:					
Organizational expenses	23,600	23,600	23,600	23,600	23,600
Operating expenses	108,000	114,480	121,349	128,630	136,348
Depreciation expenses	189,000	194,400	194,400	194,400	194,400
Total expenses:	$320,600	$332,480	$339,349	$346,630	$354,348
Profit	$399,400	$430,720	$469,643	$510,902	$554,636
Total tax liability	$111,832	$120,602	$131,500	$143,053	$161,357
Limited partners' share (99%)	$110,714	$119,396	$130,185	$141,622	$153,745

Table 9.2 (continued)

Year	6	7	8	9	10
Rental income	$963,522	$1,021,334	$1,082,614	$1,147,571	$1,216,425
Less:					
Operating expenses	144,528	153,200	162,392	172,136	182,464
Depreciation expenses	194,400	194,400	194,400	194,400	194,400
Total expenses:	$338,928	$347,600	$356,792	$366,536	$376,864
Profit	$624,594	$673,734	$725,822	$781,035	$839,561
Total tax liability	$174,886	$188,645	$203,230	$218,690	$235,077
Limited partners' share (99%)	$173,137	$186,759	$201,198	$216,503	$232,726

Table 9.3 presents the yearly tax liability for each limited partnership unit, based on each limited partner's initial contribution of $33,250. To find the tax liability per individual unit, divide the last line of Table 9.2 by the number of units (200).

Table 9.3 Yearly Tax Liability (assuming 28-percent tax bracket)

Year	Initial Outlay	Tax Liability
1	$ 33,250	$ 554
2		597
3		651
4		708
5		769
6		866
7		934
8		1,006
9		1,083
10		1,164
	$(33,250)	$6,794

Rental income less total cash disbursements (operating expenses) represent the partnership's distributive cash. The limited partner's cash flows from operations are found in Table 9.4. The last line of Table 9.4 represents the limited partners' share of the partnership's cash distribution.

Table 9.4 Cash Flow Statements

Year	1	2	3	4	5
Rental income Less:	$720,000	$763,200	$808,992	$857,532	$908,983
Operating expenses	108,000	114,480	121,349	128,630	136,348
Distributable cash	$612,000	$648,720	$687,643	$728,902	$800,096
Limited partners' share (99%)	$605,880	$642,233	$680,767	$721,613	$792,095

Year	6	7	8	9	10
Rental income Less:	$963,522	$1,021,334	$1,082,614	$1,147,571	$1,216,425
Operating expenses	144,528	153,200	162,392	172,136	182,464
Distributable cash	$818,994	$868,134	$920,222	$975,222	$1,033,961
Limited partners share	$810,804	$859,453	$911,020	$965,681	$1,023,621

Table 9.5 presents the cash distribution per limited partnership unit. Find the yearly cash flow per individual unit by dividing the last line of Table 9.5 by the number of units offered (200). The table reveals that an initial investment by the limited partner of $33,250 results in cash distributions of $40,064 during the initial 10-year period.

Disposal Stage. In addition to the cash distributions during the operating phase of the investment, the limited partners are also entitled to 99 percent of the proceeds from sale of the apartment complex. Table 9.6 shows the calculation for before-tax reversion, assuming that apartment complex is sold at the end of year ten for $13,500,000 less selling expenses of 3 percent.

Table 9.5 Yearly Cash Flow

Year	Initial Outlay	Tax Liability
1	$ 33,250	$ 3,029
2		3,211
3		3,404
4		3,608
5		3,960
6		4,054
7		4,297
8		4,555
9		4,828
10		5,118
	$(33,250)	$40,046

Table 9.6 Before-Tax Reversion

Sale price	$13,500,000
Less:	
Selling expenses	405,000
Net sale price	$13,095,000
Limited partners' cash distribution (99%)	12,964,050
Per limited partner	64,820

Each limited partner receives $64,820 ($12,964,050/200) when the asset is sold. However, each investor must still pay taxes to the extent that the cash distribution exceeds the adjusted basis.

Partner's Basis Calculations. Unlike ownership by a single individual, whose adjusted basis is original cost less accumulated depreciation, the limited partners' basis calculations are quite complex. Each partner's basis is altered by one of the following:

1. Capital contributions (increase)
2. Taxable income of the partnership (increase)

3. Borrowing by the partnership (increase)
4. Partnership losses (decrease)
5. Distributions of partnership property (decrease)
6. Reduction in amount of partnership debt (decrease)

Table 9.7 demonstrates the calculation of a limited partner's capital account. The individual partner's initial basis is an equity contribution ($33,250), and the adjusted basis is found by adding the partner's share of the partnership's profits less any cash distributions from the initial investment. Table 9.7 shows the adjusted basis as $17,450.

Table 9.7 Limited Partner's Adjusted Capital Account

(1) Year	(2) Equity Investment	(3) Profit (Loss)	(4) Cash Distribution	(5) (2 + 3 - 4) Adjusted Basis
1	$33,250	$ 1,977	$ 3,029	
2		2,132	3,211	
3		2,325	3,404	
4		2,529	3,608	
5		2,745	3,960	
6		3,093	4,054	
7		3,335	4,297	
8		3,593	4,555	
9		3,866	4,828	
10		4,156	5,118	
Totals:	$33,250	$24,264	$40,064	$17,450

Table 9.8 presents the after-tax reversion per limited partner. Each limited partner receives a cash distribution $64,820 on the sale of the apartment complex; that amount is reduced by the amount of the investor's adjusted basis of $17,450 to determine the taxable income of $47,370 from the sale. Since all investors in this project are in the 28-percent tax bracket, their individual tax liability is $13,264, which makes their net real gain is $51,556.

Table 9.8 After-Tax Reversion per Limited Partner

Cash distribution		$64,820
Less:		
Adjusted basis of limited partner		17,450
Gain on sale		$47,370
Tax liability (28% of gain)	$13,264	
After-tax reversion per limited partner	$51,556	

Table 9.9 summarizes the components of the limited partner's after-tax return. Now the limited partner's tax liability, cash distribution, and after-tax reversion is known, the after-tax return can be calculated.

Table 9.9 Limited Partner Return

Year	Sum Invested	Tax Liability	Cash Flows	Due at Reversion	Cumulative Amounts
1	$33,250	$ 554	$3,029		$(30,775)
2		597	3,211		2,614
3		651	3,404		2,753
4		708	3,608		2,900
5		769	3,960		3,191
6		866	4,054		3,188
7		934	4,297		3,363
8		1,006	4,555		3,549
9		1,083	4,828		3,745
10		1,164	5,118	$51,556	55,510
Total					$50,038

IRR = 14.3%
NPV_{12} = $4,494

The investor's after-tax return or internal rate of return (IRR) is 14.26 percent, and the net present value at 12 percent is $4,494.

Summary

Apartment rental properties offer excellent opportunities for above-average investment returns, whether the ownership is direct or through a limited partnership. The underlying fundamentals suggest the possibility of strong earnings increases for this type of property. Improving cash flows from apartment rentals increase potential for appreciation in the value of the investment. These changes increases the likelihood that the investor will earn a superior rate of return in this area.

The anticipated good prospects for rental properties arise from both supply and demand factors. The Tax Reform Act of 1986 has diminished enthusiasm for this type of investment, resulting in a smaller increase in supply than the fundamentals would suggest. The demand for apartment rentals is expected to increase throughout the next decade and beyond as a result of changing demographics, changing lifestyles, and relative increases in the price of single-family housing.

Chapter 10

Condominiums

Condominiums provide attractive investment vehicles in real estate for many people. Most people think of condominiums as multifamily dwellings located primarily in vacation areas. In fact, the term condominium refers to the form of ownership, rather than the type of real estate. All types of real estate can be held in condominium form: single-family residential, multifamily housing, office buildings, warehouses and even boat slips in marinas. This chapter focuses on condominiums that are units in multifamily dwellings.

Condominiums are created when the value of this form of ownership exceeds the value of ownership in some other form. A common example is the owner of an apartment building who finds it advantageous to convert building to a number of individually-owned units. Splitting a single entity into individual units may increase the value of the property because the units offer ownership amenity and consequent tax advantages or because this form of ownership yields access to a more favorable market.

As an example of the latter, suppose the owner of a 50-unit apartment complex on a beach in a desirable resort can sell the complex as an entity for $5,000,000 ($100,000/CPU) or as 50 individual units for $150,000 each. The choice the developer or owner would make is clear.

Another way property may be divided is according to time. Under a time-sharing arrangement, property rights are delineated by date as well as place. The rights of time-sharing property owners are specified by the relevant state statutes and vary considerably from state to state. The relative newness of the concept of time-sharing properties generally means that they are not good for investment purposes.

Condominiums have much to recommend them to an investor. They tend to be less expensive than comparable individually-owned properties, are a relatively liquid form of real estate investment, and and have limited maintenance responsibilities since exterior maintenance is generally the responsibility of the homeowners association. For many condominiums, a rental or real estate agency serves the majority of owners.

117

Condominium ownership has some disadvantages: cash flow may be diminished by condominium fee assessments, the homeowners association may set rules for the use of individual units, and the market for condominiums in a particular area may be overdeveloped by aggressive builders putting downward pressure on price.

Condominium ownership may offer the investor great opportunities for profit. This form of ownership is neither inherently good or bad. As with other real estate opportunities, a careful analysis of cash inflows and outflows over time is necessary to assess the desirability of the investment.

Ownership System

In a condominium, an investor buys an individual unit of the development plus a share of the common area. The common area may include hallways, walkways, open areas, swimming pools, parking lots, and even golf courses. The management of the condominium is often directed by trustees elected by individual members of the homeowners association. Homeowners association bylaws normally detail the duties and responsibilities of the trustees. The trustees then set forth rules and regulations for the association and assess fees on individual units to cover costs.

Financing

Most financial institutions treat condominium financing exactly as they do the financing of conventional real estate. Since the condominium form is often used primarily to benefit the builder or owner of a new condominium, the builder or owner often provides special financing to buyers. These special arrangements can often be of great advantage to the buyer. Those advantages often take the form of less money down or lower than market interest rates. Frequently, the seller agrees to pick up the first year's condominium fees.

Evaluating Condominiums

Homeowners Association

The homeowners association has a great deal of responsibility and power. When purchasing a unit in an ongoing association, an investor must evaluate the association's financial condition. If it has not established adequate reserves for maintenance, a big special assessment may be looming around the corner.

The rules and regulations of the association should also be carefully examined. Condominium bylaws frequently prohibit leasing the units for periods of less than one year. Some have an outright prohibition against leasing. Parking rights, pool rights, children, pets, and almost every other factor affecting the use of the units may be covered by the association bylaws. The association bylaws are an extremely important factor in determining the desirability of investing in a given condominium.

Rental Desirability
A single-family condominium unit's desirability as a rental unit is affected by the same factors that determine the desirability of a single-family house or apartment unit for this purpose (see Chapters 7 and 8).

If the condominium is located in a resort area, investors need basic information—length of the season, rental rates, and expected vacancy rate—to calculate expected revenues. Prudent investors do not rely on sellers as an exclusive source of such information. Independent real estate agents may provide an unbiased source of information on these subjects.

Appreciation Potential
Where the condominium is used as a residence and not located in a resort area, the factors that influence its potential to appreciate are very much like those of single-family residences (see Chapter 7); however, a few important differences exist. Single-family housing generally rises in price, given some demand factor, because the supply of land is fixed and building costs rise. Condominiums are much less land-intensive. The effective supply of condominiums in a given market is much more elastic than the supply of single-family homes. This situation can lead to both greater short-term volatility in condominium prices and less long-term appreciation.

The tendency to short-run volatility in resort areas is even greater. Condominiums in resorts frequently face a demand which is not particularly sensitive to price. This can mean a succession of situations in which condominium prices are either abnormally low or abnormally high. Investors should carefully assess the price of a unit in terms of the cycle of prices in order to maximize the potential for appreciation.

General Investment Characteristics

Strengths

Low Unit Price. Condominium units tend to be more affordable than comparable, traditional individually-owned housing units. This is largely because condominiums are frequently grouped in multifamily buildings, which have lower unit costs because of construction economies. Amenities such as pools, open spaces, and a clubhouse that tend to be too expensive when the entire cost is born by an individual are quite affordable when the cost is shared.

Liquidity. The market for condominiums is often quite liquid, with a high proportion of transactions relative to the total stock of such housing.

Ease of Maintenance. The homeowners association takes responsibility for exterior building and grounds maintenance. In the townhouse-style condominiums, individual owners may have some of this responsibility.

Potential Savings on Finance. A condominium's builder or developer sometimes offers special financing arrangements to buyers. This may take the form of a lower interest rate, called a *buydown.* The builder effectively purchases the lower interest rate from a lending institution. Buydowns are usually of limited duration.

Weaknesses

Condominium Fee. The homeowners association assesses a fee to cover exterior and grounds maintenance and to provide for common services or expenses as necessary. These reduce the income and cash flow associated with the investment. Condominium fees may be increased by the board of trustees. Investors should investigate the association's finances to see whether the current fee structure is realistic. More than one investor has been surprised by a dramatic increase in condominium fees shortly after buying in.

Loss of Control. The ability of investors to use the property for their intended purposes is at the discretion of the bylaws of the homeowners association.

Price Volatility. The ability of the supply of condominiums to respond (and even over-respond) to market conditions can result in substantial short-term price fluctuations. The absence of the uniqueness that characterizes single-family homes tends to further exaggerate these fluctuations. Small movements in supply or demand can severely impact the liquidity of an investment in a condominium.

Tax Considerations

The tax treatment of condominium units as real estate investments is generally the same as for single-family dwellings (see Chapter 8). One difference lies in the existence of condominium fees, which lower income and cash flow but are offset by some additional tax savings.

Case Study

Acquisition Phase. Suppose an investor purchases a beachfront condominium for $180,000, with land costs of $20,000 and closing costs of $8,000. With 20 percent down, the seller agrees to finance the balance for 30 years with an interest rate of 7 percent the first year, 8 percent the second year, 9 percent the third year, and 10 percent per year thereafter. These circumstances are specified in Table 10.1.

Table 10.1 Source and Use of Funds Statement

Sources of funds	
Debt	$150,400
Equity	37,600
Total sources	$188,000
Uses of funds	
Land cost	$ 20,000
Condo cost	160,000
Closing costs	8,000
Total uses	$188,000

Holding Phase. The condominium's fees are $140 per month for the first year, expected to increase 6 percent per year. Taxes are $3,500 per year, expected to increase 5 percent per year. In the fifth year, the owner receives a special $2,000 pool repair assessment.

Rental income ranges from $1,200 per week at the height of the season to $100 per week in the least popular time. First-year revenues net of leasing costs are expected to total $20,000 given anticipated vacancy rates and to increase yearly at 8 percent from this level.

These assumptions create a net income ranging from $3,500 in year one to $20,554 in year ten (see Table 10.2). The increase in profits is largely fueled by the escalating rental revenues.

Table 10.2 Income Statement Condominium Project

Year	1	2	3	4	5
Rental income	20,000	21,600	23,328	25,194	27,210
Operating Ex					
Taxes	$3,500	$3,675	$3,859	$4,052	$4,254
Condo fee	1,680	1,781	1,888	2,001	2,121
Special fees	0	0	0	0	2,000
Depr	5,600	5,760	5,760	5,760	5,760
Interest	10,480	11,861	13,227	14,578	14,462
Profit (loss)	$3,920	$3,979	$4,341	$4,856	$6,988
Taxes	$1,098	$1,114	$1,215	$1,360	$1,957

Year	6	7	8	9	10
Rental income	29,387	31,737	34,276	37,019	39,980
Operating Ex					
Taxes	$4,467	$4,690	$4,925	$5,171	$5,430
Condo fee	2,248	2,383	2,526	2,678	2,838
Special fees	0	0	0	0	0
Depr	5,760	5,760	5,760	5,760	5,760
Interest	14,333	14,190	14,032	13,858	13,666
Profit (loss)	$9,294	$11,787	$14,484	$17,401	$20,554
Taxes	$2,602	$3,300	$4,056	$4,872	$5,755

The cash low levels illustrated in Table 10.3 are considerably larger than the income flows depicted in Table 10.2. The reason for this lies in the extent to which depreciation shelters income. Note, this effect diminishes in later years as the mortgage is paid down.

Table 10.3 Cash Flow Statement Condominium Project

Year	1	2	3	4	5
Rental income	20,000	21,600	23,328	25,194	27,210
Total	$20,000	$21,600	$23,328	$25,194	$27,210
Operating Ex					
Taxes	$3,500	$3,675	$3,859	$4,052	$4,254
Condo fee	1,680	1,781	1,888	2,001	2,121
Special fees	0	0	0	0	2,000
Debt Service	12,007	13,219	14,450	15,696	15,696
Cash Flow	$7,993	$8,381	$8,878	$9,498	$11,514

Year	6	7	8	9	10
Rental income	29,387	31,737	34,276	37,019	39,980
Total	$29,387	$31,737	$34,276	$37,019	$39,980
Operating Ex					
Taxes	$4,467	$4,690	$4,925	$5,171	$5,430
Condo fee	2,248	2,383	2,526	2,678	2,838
Special fees	0	0	0	0	0
Debt Service	15,696	15,696	15,696	15,696	15,696
Cash Flow	$13,691	$16,041	$18,580	$21,323	$24,284

Disposal Phase. The investor holds the condominium ten years and then sells at $400,000 (less $40,000 real estate commissions and closing costs).

The basis calculation is specified in Table 10.4. The adjusted basis is $130,560. Given the net asset sale price of $360,000, an investor in the 28-percent tax bracket has a tax liability of $64,243 and net income of $165,197 (see Table 10.5).

The after-tax cash flow of $160,217 is depicted in Table 10.6.

Table 10.4 Basic Calculation

Cost of property	$188,000
Less depreciation	57,440
Adjusted basis	$130,560

Table 10.5 Tax Schedule

Net sales	$360,000
Adjusted basis	130,560
Gain on sale	$229,440
Tax liability (28% of gain)	64,243
Net income	$165,197

Table 10.6 After-Tax Cash Flow

Selling price	$400,000
Less:	
Selling commission	40,000
Mortgage balance	135,540
Taxes	64,243
Net cash flow	$165,197

The profitability of the investment is detailed in Table 10.7. Evaluating the cash flow over the 10-year period at a 15-percent rate of discount yields a net present value of $126,725. This translates into an internal rate of return of almost 31 percent.

Table 10.7 Investment Evaluation

Year	Cash Flow		Taxes	Total
0	$(37,600)			$(37,600)
1	7,993		$1,098	6,895
2	8,381		1,114	7,267
3	8,878		1,215	7,663
4	9,498		1,360	8,138
5	11,514		1,957	9,557
6	13,691		2,602	11,088
7	16,041		3,300	12,741
8	18,580		4,056	14,525
9	21,323		4,872	16,450
10	24,284	160,217	5,755	178,746
	$140,183		$27,329	$273,071

IRR = 30.9%
NPV_{15} = $126,725

Summary

Condominiums as investment opportunities have a number of distinct advantages and disadvantages. The relatively small capital required, in combination with the liquidity of the investment and the ease of maintenance, recommend this form of investment to a novice or cautious investor. The presence of value derived from the amenity value of ownership in a resort situation has resulted in great popularity for this form of investment.

Two specific problems investors should be wary of are the possibility of a homeowners association restricting the owners' ability to lease the property and the possibility of buying at the wrong stage of the property value cycle. Either circumstance severely curtails the desirability of a particular condominium as an investment.

Chapter 11

CHAPTER 11

Undeveloped Land

The acquisition of undeveloped land for potential appreciation is very attractive emotionally. The ownership of undeveloped land appears to yield investors psychic income having to do with "owning" a piece of America and dreams of great wealth. This appeal is a dangerous one. Historically, waves of speculative fever in undeveloped land have occurred to trap the unwary investor.

Investment in undeveloped land has been the key to many fortunes in the United States. Hundreds of thousands of investors of all sizes have made money investing in undeveloped real estate. These investors have been rewarded for their foresight and persistence and have benefitted from shifting land use patterns and economic growth. Investors today face similar opportunities.

Investing in undeveloped land combines high returns with high risk. Where the possibility for an alternative use of undeveloped land is known, the value of that potential appreciation is built into the price of the land. Where the potential for undeveloped land is not recognized, and consequently not expressed in its price, realizing a gain in value is fraught with uncertainty and hazard. What will eventually happen to the land depends on a host of unknown eventualities: the future rate of national growth, the pattern of urban development, the availability of capital, the location of industry, the cost of transportation, land use restrictions, zoning laws, the location of future roads, the location of future public utilities. Further, the difficulties of successfully investing in undeveloped land are compounded by the general absence of opportunities for leverage and tax advantages found in other real estate investments.

Investing in undeveloped land is an aggressive strategy that investors should undertake only if they have adequate financial resources to pursuing an unwavering vision of the future.

General Investment Characteristics

Strengths

Appreciation from Shifting Land Use. The potential for appreciation of undeveloped land arises from either or both a shift in land use or the dis-aggregation of a large property into smaller pieces. A 40-acre tract in a rural area with no residential use apparent as a consequence of its isolated location may be purchased for $20,000. The unanticipated construction of a major road connecting this area to a nearby urban center may cause the value of this land to increase as it can be shifted to residential use. Then the land can be sold to a developer for $5,000 an acre (for a total of $200,000). The developer would prepare the property for residential use by grading, clearing, building roads, installing utilities, etc., and sell perhaps fifty lots at $20,000 (for a total of $1,000,000). Either action under the for-tuitous circumstances described results in significant appreciation.

Fixed Supply. It may be argued that land will always go up in value be-cause of its fixed supply in the face of continuous economic growth. The fifty states comprise some fifty billion acres of land. About eight acres of land per person in the United States. Of this, about three acres per person are arable. Each year environmental concerns, zoning laws, new homes, roads, shopping centers, and a variety of industrial, commercial, and public buildings eat up a portion of the stock of undeveloped land.

Inflation. Land prices may be thought to rise from general inflationary pressures. Over the past two decades, consumer prices have increased more than 120 percent. In 1967, the average new home sold for $23,000. In comparison, the average new home sold today costs over $100,000. Land, as a proportion of the total cost of a new home, has risen steadily throughout this period. As with other scarce resources, land prices have risen dramatically in those areas that have experienced economic growth.

Weaknesses

Predicting Land Value. Whatever general trends occur, each property is unique. Increases in land values are not uniformly distributed. The value of land in a region may rise or fall as a result of unpredictable events. The fuel oil shortage and consequent energy cost increase shifted population from the Northeast and Upper Midwest to the Sunbelt in the 1980s. The rise in the cost of gasoline changed commutation patterns in urban areas. The fall in fuel oil prices in the 1980s devastated land prices in Texas. The continuing depression in agriculture has prolonged the migration from rural to urban America.

Regional patterns in land use depend on a variety of macroeconomic, demographic, sociological, and industrial trends. Within a region, whatever overall trends may appear, considerable variation occurs between individual property uses. These are affected by specific land use regulations, zoning laws, road patterns, the availability of public utilities, the location of public services, and prior land use patterns. Even within highly developed urban areas it is not unusual to find substantial undeveloped land. Why is some land used and some bypassed? Accurately predicting the future value of undeveloped land calls for both skill and luck.

Determining the value of undeveloped land is difficult. Even experts in the field frequently disagree. In general, the market for undeveloped land is not liquid, and no comparables exist from which to estimate value. Past prices for land in similar use is irrelevant in the face of an anticipated change in land use patterns.

Future land use (and hence price) for a specific property is difficult to predict because of the many factors impacting land use. Growth in a region, or even in the local area, does not necessarily imply the value of a specific property will increase. A new plant may come to town, attracting many workers and causing a general rise in property value. To accommodate the increased population the town may decide to build a new sewer plant adjacent to any given property, causing its value to decline.

Speculation. Volatility in the price of undeveloped land is occasionally fueled by speculative fever. Many investors are prone to elastic expectations. Such investors feel the most important determinant of future prices are recent price changes. They feel that a recent history of price increases is indicative of future price increases, irrespective of the fundamentals.

Under those circumstances investors purchase property knowing the price exceeds the property's "worth" but with the expectation that some other buyer will pay even more. This is also known as the "bigger fool" theory. This is a dangerous strategy and on it has foundered many a hope and dream.

Carrying Costs. The difficulty in successfully investing in undeveloped land is compounded by carrying costs that are not offset by an income stream. There are two types of carrying costs. Explicit carrying costs require cash outlay: property taxes, land assessment fees, and any finance costs actually expended. Implicit costs arise from opportunities that could have been pursued had capital not been tied up in a real estate project. The internal rate of return and net present value concepts developed in Chapter 3 allow the direct comparison of the effective return with implicit and explicit costs. For example, if the internal rate of return on a project is 12 percent and the capital employed in that project could have earned 10 percent elsewhere, the true return from the project is 2 percent.

This approach provides a powerful perspective for real estate investors. It suggests that the acquisition of undeveloped land with substantial carrying costs that needs to be held a long time to realize a rise in value cannot be evaluated in simplistic terms.

Leverage. One of the most significant advantages in real estate investing is the opportunity to use leverage. As explained in Chapter 3, the net effect of this practice is to make capital work harder. Unfortunately, capital from conventional financing sources for undeveloped land is limited, if available at all. Bankers look with disfavor on proposals to finance undeveloped property and other non-income-producing properties. They also tend to view as speculative those properties characterized by negative cash flow for some indeterminate time in the hope of unknown eventualities. Financing for undeveloped property, when available, has a much lower loan-to-value ratio and is of shorter duration than that for developed property.

An alternative source of funds may be found in the seller of the property. In order to secure a sale at the desired price, the seller may be willing to use some or all of his equity to finance the purchase. Much depends on the investor's negotiating skill and the seller's need to move quickly.

An alternative to purchasing property outright is to secure an option. An *option* is so named because it is a contract between the buyer and seller that grants the buyer the right (or option) to purchase the property at some specified price over some specific period of time in exchange for consideration. Options may be assignable or not assignable. Use of an assignable option significantly reduces an investor's need for capital and transactions cost.

The use of an option may significantly increase the investor's leverage and reduce carrying costs. However, obtaining an option at a reasonable price for a sufficiently long period of time may be difficult.

Liquidity. Undeveloped land is one of the least liquid types of real estate property. This may cause a problem for investors who tend to use their investments as stores of value. Shares in a large, actively-traded REIT or MLP, can be converted into cash liquidated with little loss of value. Liquidity arises from the relatively low transactions cost and an active buyer's market. Investors who hold undeveloped land and for some unanticipated reason want to convert the investment into cash incur much higher transaction costs and may be confronted with a scarcity of buyers. Under these circumstances, the only way to become liquid would be to take a substantial loss.

Tax Considerations

Many of the tax advantages of investing in developed real estate do not transfer to undeveloped real estate. Raw land, for example, cannot be depreciated. Losses from interest expenses, acquisition costs, and other associated expenses cannot be used to offset earned income to reduce tax liability—with the sole exception of property tails.

In eliminating the capital gains tax, the Tax Reform Act of 1986 reduced the advantages long-term investments whose profits were not taxed until they were realized compared to earning income in a steady stream over time. This does not make the investment in undeveloped land necessarily unattractive, but it does reduce the former attractiveness of this form of investment relative to other forms of real estate investment.

Case Study

Acquisition Phase. The undeveloped land used in this case study is a 20-acre parcel located on the interchange of a major interstate highway in a rural area. The investor envisions that this property will one day have commercial value that will arise from the continued development of two major urban centers that are connected by the highway. It is felt that within ten years traffic will increase sufficiently to sustain gas stations, a motel, and a small shopping center. The land is currently zoned for this type of commercial use.

The land is acquired from its present owner for $100,000 with $50,000 cash up front and interest-only at 12 percent on the balance which must be paid off in 10 years or less.

Table 11.1 Sources and Used of Funds

Sources of funds	
Equity	$ 50,000
Debt	50,000
	$100,000
Uses of funds	
Land	$100,000

Holding Phase. Property taxes are currently $2,000 per year but estimated to increase at five percent per year. The investor, aware that carrying costs not offset by income can seriously erode the profitability of a project of this type. The investor therefore finds three small businesses that can make appropriate use of the land until its commercial potential is fulfilled. Acerage is leased to a small farmer for a vegetable and produce stand, to another party for a miniature golf stand, and a third party for a fireworks stand. Initial rent totals only $1,500 per year but is expected to increase 20 percent per year as traffic builds.

Table 11.2 contains the combined income and cash flows for this project under these assumptions. As is typical for an investment in undeveloped land, cash flow is negative throughout the life of the project. Note that although tax savings occur, losses are not fully applicable against ordinary income resulting in suspended loses.

Disposal Phase. During the ten-year period, the investor was increasingly sought out by commercial principals interested in the land. In order to maximize the sale price of the property, the investor rejected such interest. At the end of the ten-year period, there were many eager potential buyers for the property. The investor then sold the property in four separate parcels for $660,000, of which the investor nets $600,000.

The gain on the property is the net sale price less cumulative suspended losses and the initial cost of the property (Table 11.3). Table 11.4 (page 136) indicates a net after-tax cash flow of $415,897. Adjusting for the negative cash flow and tax savings yields an absolute return of $326,723 (Table 11.5, page 136).

Table 11.2 Consolidated Income and Cash Flow Statement Undeveloped Land Project

Year	1	2	3	4	5
Rent	$1,500	$1,800	$2,160	$2,592	$3,110
Less:					
Property tax	$2,000	$2,100	$2,205	$2,315	$2,431
Interest	6,000	6,000	6,000	6,000	6,000
Cash flow	($6,500)	($6,300)	($6,045)	($5,723)	($5,321)
Tax saving	$560	$588	$617	$648	$681
Suspended					
losses	($4,500)	($4,200)	($3,840)	($3,408)	($2,890)

Year	6	7	8	9	10
Rent	$3,732	$4,479	$5,375	$6,450	$7,740
Less:					
Property tax	$2,553	$2,680	$2,814	$2,955	$3,103
Interest	6,000	6,000	6,000	6,000	6,000
Cash flow	($4,820)	($4,201)	($3,439)	($2,505)	($1,363)
Tax saving	$715	$750	$788	$827	$869
Suspended					
losses	($2,268)	($1,521)	$625	$450	($1,740)

Table 11.3 Tax Liability Analysis

Net sale price	$600,000
Less:	
Suspended losses	21,062
Cost of land	100,000
Gain on sale	$478,938
Tax liability (28% of gain)	$134,103

Table 11.4 After-Tax Cash Flow

Sale price	$660,000
Less:	
Mortgage balance	50,000
Closing costs	60,000
Tax liability	134,103
Net after-tax cash flow	$415,897

Table 11.5 Evaluation of Return

Year	Cash Flow	Tax Savings	Total CF & TS
0	$(50,000)		$(50,000)
1	(6,500)	$ 560	(5,940)
2	(6,300)	588	(5,712)
3	(6,045)	617	(5,428)
4	(5,723)	648	(5,075)
5	(5,321)	681	(4,640)
6	(4,820)	715	(4,105)
7	(4,201)	750	(3,451)
8	(3,439)	788	(2,651)
9	(2,505)	827	(1,678)
10	(1,363)	869	$415,403
Totals	$(96,217)	$7,043	$326,723

IRR = 19.5%
NPV_{21} = –$7,379

The project shows a modest 19.5 IRR despite a more than 500-percent increase in value of the property over a ten-year period. This result from the effect of the negative cash flow that occurs continuously throughout the period and the effect of the discounting mechanism on revenues received far in the future. Had this investor not been able to find some income-producing activity for the project, the IRR would have been barely positive.

The use of a 21-percent rate of discount in the net present value calculation generates a negative NPV of $7,379. This suggests a project should not be undertaken if the risk factor warrants the use of a 21-percent discount rate.

The use of 21-percent rate of discount is appropriate for the risk inherent in investing in undeveloped land. Indeed, where this book uses a 12-percent rate of discount for conservative real estate investments (single-family housing and apartments), it would not be inappropriate for conservative investors to use a much higher rate of discount than 21 percent. The land might have lost its zoning classification, the expected traffic might never have developed because competing roads were constructed, developers might have shown a distinct preference for developing the next interchange down the road. Each of these events would probably have lowered the value of the land sufficiently for the investor to take an absolute loss. The uncertainty inherent in undeveloped land investment warrants a substantial rate of discount to protect the investor from exposure to risk.

Summary

Investment in undeveloped land offers considerable potential to sophisticated investors with pockets deep enough to protect them from liquidity problems and to carry the project through to fruition. This potential often misleads investors because the costs of carrying the property over time are not adequately considered or because the inherent risks associated with the investment are not taken sufficiently into account. Accurately analyzing the potential profit in undeveloped land requires careful consideration of all cash flows and their timing.

A danger to potential investors in undeveloped land is getting caught up in the psychological frenzy of a speculative bubble. Undeveloped land is usually undeveloped for good reason. Success in this type of investment requires the ability to anticipate a shift in land use patterns before this change is perceived by the market. Investing in undeveloped land is one area where excessive enthusiasm is a real danger.

Chapter 12

Rehabilitation Properties

Current tax law provides special incentives for real estate projects that use old or historic buildings under certain conditions. Investors can significantly enhance the return on a real estate investment project by acquiring or remodeling an old or historic building as part of that project.

This chapter discusses special tax treatment applicable to single-family residences, apartments, office buildings, industrial facilities, commercial facilities, and low-income housing. The U.S. government provides specific tax incentives to encourage the rehabilitation of historic property for other than personal residential purposes since 1976.

These tax incentives provide significant opportunities for investors to obtain an above average return. The tax law distinguishes between buildings that are merely old (built prior to 1936) and historic buildings. Rehabilitations of the latter receive greater tax benefits.

Old Buildings

A one-time tax credit equal to 10 percent of rehabilitation costs may be claimed on buildings originally placed in service prior to 1936, providing certain original structural requirements are met. These tax credits may be applied on a dollar-for-dollar basis against the tax on passive income or against the tax on ordinary income, up to a limit of $8,333 for a taxpayer subject to the five-percent surcharge. The original structural requirements provisions require that the building retain 75 percent of its internal structural framework and 50 percent of its external walls as external walls or retain at least 75 percent of its exterior walls as exterior walls.

Any tax credit earned must be subtracted from the depreciable base of the property. Unused tax credits may be carried forward.

Historic Buildings

A one-time tax credit equal to 20 percent of the cost of rehabilitation may be realized if the property is "historic" and meets the original structural requirements for old buildings. A property may qualify as "historic" in two ways: by being located in an area certified by the state as being a historic district or by being listed on the National Register of Historical Landmarks.

The Register is maintained by the U.S. Department of the Interior. To apply for a listing in the Register, an investor should contact the Historic Preservation Officer in the state in which the project is located. One of the duties of this officer is to guide applicants through the historic designation process. This process normally involves a formal review by experts in the field of historic architecture.

A property so designated may be used as a place of business or leased for commercial purposes as long as the historic value of the property is not impaired. An investor may not use the property as a personal residence. Any tax credit granted is deducted from the depreciable basis of the property.

General Investment Characteristics

Strengths

Higher Return from Tax Reduction. Historic properties are depreciated in the same manner as any other residential or nonresidential property. As a result of the expense of rehabilitation and restoration, a relatively greater proportion of the building's value may be in its depreciable basis. The property will thus yield a greater tax shelter, other things being equal.

The 20-percent tax credit is a dollar-for-dollar reduction in tax liability. This differs significantly from an income offset: in the 28-percent tax bracket, $1 of tax credit is equivalent to $3.57 of depreciation. The tax credit can be applied only against $25,000 of ordinary income, resulting in a maximum tax saving in any one year of $8,333, for individuals subject to the five-percent surcharge. There is no limitation on the tax credit that can be applied against tax liability arising from passive income.

Higher Returns from Unique Property. As with any investment, investors balance potential returns on investment in old or historic buildings with potential risks. The project envisioned must be economically viable in terms of price, location, and the relevant characteristics of the real estate market. Historic properties in urban areas are often undervalued because they have deteriorated into unsightly condition or are located in unattractive neighborhoods. Such property often has a highly desirable location in urban areas that are just beginning to be redeveloped.

A properly refurbished building may derive considerable value as a commercial property because of its historic attributes. In an era of urban homesteading, such property may also have significant potential for appreciation.

Weaknesses

Expense of Historical Designation. The process of obtaining designation of a property as an historical site may require expensive legal services. Once a designation is secured, maintaining the building's historical identity may require additional architectural or building expenses.

Loss of Control. Historical designation means that the property owner agrees to share the property rights with the larger community, in some sense. Plans for use of the building and the exact nature of the rehabilitation may be subject to review by community groups. Decisions about architectural characteristics, additional refurbishing, maintenance, use, and the selection of tenants may no longer be the unilateral prerogative of the property owner. The need for community consensus on such matters is specified in the legal historical designation papers.

Cost Control. The difficulties inherent in historical rehabilitation work are difficult to forecast. Completion of an historical rehabilitation may exceed anticipated costs because of structural problems that were not apparent when work was begun or because the nature of the problem of maintaining the building's historic value was not correctly anticipated.

Tax Considerations
The Tax Reform Act of 1986 diminished but did not eliminate incentives for historic rehabilitation. Lengthening the depreciation period, requiring straight-line depreciation, lowering of marginal tax brackets, and eliminating capital gains reduced the attractiveness of many forms of real estate investment. This has made the use of the historic rehabilitation provisions more attractive than ever, relative to standard tax treatment.

Case Study

Acquisition Phase. The rehabilitation tax credit applies to many different types of real estate properties, so the hypothetical historic rehabilitation project we discuss here is rather generic in form, to demonstrate the financial incentives of the relevant provisions of the tax code.

Table 12.1 presents a schedule of the initial sources and uses of funds for the project. The property cost is $30,000, settlement costs (including mortgage points) are estimated to be $7,000, and rehabilitation costs are expected to run $78,000 for a total cost of $115,000.

Table 12.1 Sources and Uses of Funds

Capital required:	
Cost of land	$ 7,500
Cost of building	22,500
Renovation costs	78,000
Points (3%)	2,640
Additional closing costs	4,360
Total capital required:	$115,000
Sources of capital	
Mortgage (10% for 30 years)	$ 88,000
Investor's capital	27,000
Total capital provided:	$115,000

Holding Phase. The investor puts up $27,000 in equity, secures the balance with a mortgage for $88,000 amortized over 30 years at 10 percent per year (see Table 12.2 for amortization), and plans to hold the property for 10 years. The total annual debt servicing requirement is $9,267.12.

Table 12.2 shows the annual interest expense, and the investor can write off mortgage points over the 30-year amortization also ($2,640/30). The depreciation expense in the first year is calculated by multiplying the appropriate depreciation percentage (3.5 percent) by the sum of the cost of the existing structure ($22,500) plus 80 percent of the rehabilitation expenditures ($78,000), for a total for $2,972 (.035 times $84,900). For each subsequent year of the holding period, the depreciation percentage is 3.6, which gives the investor a depreciation expense of $3,056 for each year.

Table 12.2 Loan Amortization Schedule $88,000 30-Year Loan (10 percent)

Year	Total Interest	Principal Payment	Total Payment	Remaining Balance
1	$8,777.98	$ 489.14	$9,267.12	$87,510.87
2	8,726.79	540.33	9,267.12	86,970.52
3	8,670.17	596.95	9,267.12	86,373.58
4	8,607.68	659.44	9,267.12	85,714.15
5	8,538.61	728.51	9,267.12	84,985.64
6	8,462.33	804.79	9,267.12	84,180.86
7	8,378.08	889.04	9,267.12	83,291.82
8	8,284.99	982.13	9,267.12	82,309.69
9	8,182.14	1,084.98	9,267.12	81,224.70
10	8,068.53	1,198.59	9,267.12	80,026.12
11	7,943.01	1,324.11	9,267.12	78,702.00
12	7,804.37	1,462.75	9,267.12	77,239.25
13	7,651.20	1,615.92	9,267.12	75,623.34
14	7,481.99	1,785.13	9,267.12	73,838.21
15	7,295.07	1,972.05	9,267.12	71,866.16
16	7,088.53	2,178.59	9,267.12	69,687.56
17	6,860.43	2,406.69	9,267.12	67,280.85
18	6,608.42	2,658.70	9,267.12	64,622.15
19	6,330.03	2,937.09	9,267.12	61,685.07
20	6,022.47	3,244.65	9,267.12	58,440.42
21	5,682.71	3,584.41	9,267.12	54,856.01
22	5,307.39	3,959.73	9,267.12	50,896.28
23	4,892.74	4,374.38	9,267.12	46,521.90
24	4,434.69	4,832.43	9,267.12	41,689.47
25	3,928.65	5,338.47	9,267.12	36,351.00
26	3,369.63	5,897.49	9,267.12	30,453.50
27	2,752.12	6,515.00	9,267.12	23,938.50
28	2,069.92	7,197.20	9,267.12	16,741.30
29	1,316.26	7,950.86	9,267.12	8,790.45
30	483.71	8,790.45	9,274.16	0

Table 12.3 shows the forecast income over the 10-year holding period. Rental income is $12,960 the first year with 3-percent annual increases. Operating expenses are forecast at 15-percent of each year's annual income.

Taxable income or loss represents rental income less the sum of operating expenses, depreciation, interest expense, and points. The rehabilitation tax credit is $15,600, which is 20 percent of the renovation cost ($78,000). In year one, the tax effect equals 28 percent of the loss (-$882) or $230 plus the rehabilitation tax credit of $15,600 for a total tax benefit of $15,830. (This calculation assumes the investor has enough passive income to use the entire amount of tax credits and losses in year one; if the investor has no passive income, the tax benefit is limited to $8,333 per year.) In subsequent years, the tax effect is found by multiplying the investor's taxable loss (or profit) by 28 percent.

Table 12.3 Income Statement—Real Estate Project

Year	1	2	3	4	5
Rental income	$12,960	$13,349	$13,749	$14,587	$14,587
Less:					
Operating expenses	1,944	2,002	2,062	2,124	2,188
Depreciation	2,972	3,056	3,056	3,056	3,056
Interest expense	8,778	8,727	8,670	8,608	8,539
Points	88	88	88	88	88
Profit (loss)	−822	−525	−128	285	715
RTC	15,600				
Tax effect	$15,830	$ 147	$ 36	−$ 80	$ 715

Year	6	7	8	9	10
Rental income	$15,024	$15,475	$15,939	$16,417	$16,910
Less:					
Operating expenses	2,254	2,321	2,391	2,463	2,536
Interest expense	8,462	8,378	8,285	8,182	8,069
Depreciation expense	3,056	3,056	3,056	3,056	3,056
Points	88	88	88	88	88
Profit (loss)	1,164	1,631	2,119	2,628	3,160
Tax effect (28%)	−$326	−$457	−$593	−$736	−$885

The investor's net cash flow for the project is determined by subtracting the sum of operating expenses and debt servicing requirements from rental income. The rehabilitation project's cash flow improves through time since the debt servicing requirements (by far the largest cash outflow) are fixed, while both rental income and operating expenses increase by three percent per year (see Table 12.4).

Table 12.4 Cash Flow Statement—Real Estate Project

Year	1	2	3	4	5
Rental income	$12,960	$13,349	$13,749	$14,587	$14,587
Less:					
Operating expenses	1,944	2,002	2,062	2,124	2,188
Debt service	9,267	9,267	9,267	9,267	9,267
Cash flow	$789	$1,091	$1,401	$1,721	$2,051

Year	6	7	8	9	10
Rental income	$15,024	$15,475	$15,939	$16,417	$16,910
Less:					
Operating expenses	2,254	2,321	2,391	2,463	2,536
Debt service	9,267	9,267	9,267	9,267	9,267
Cash flow	$2,391	$2,740	$3,101	$3,472	$3,854

Disposal Phase. The property appreciates at three percent per year over the 10-year holding period and sells for $145,152, with closing costs of five percent. To determine the tax liability and resulting after-tax cash flow, however, the investor must determine the property's basis (the initial price plus nonexpensed closing costs less the sum of annual depreciation expenses over the holding period). (See Table 12.5.)

Table 12.5 Basis Calculation

Acquisition costs	$108,000
Plus:	
Closing costs	7,000
	$115,000
Less:	
Accumulated depreciation	30,479
Points written off	880
Adjusted basis	$ 83,641

To determine tax liability, the investor first subtracts the adjusted basis ($83,641) from the net sale price (gross sale price minus closing costs) to find taxable income of $54,254, which is subject to the investor's 28-percent tax rate. Tax liability is $15,191 (as shown in Table 12.6).

Table 12.6 Tax Liability

Net sale price		$137,894
Less:		
Adjusted basis		83,641
Taxable income		$ 54,254
Tax liability (at 28%)	$ 15,191	

Having established the tax liability, the investor finds the after-tax cash flow by subtracting the sum of closing costs, mortgage balance ($80,026; see Table 12.7), and taxes from the gross sale price. The after-tax cash flow is $42,677.

The after-tax rate of return is composed of three components: the project's cash flow during the investment phase, the tax effects over the holding phase, and the after-tax reversion. (See Table 12.8.)

Table 12.7 After-Tax Cash Flow

Selling price	$145,152
Less:	
Selling expenses (5%)	$ 7,258
Mortgage balance	80,026
Tax liability	15,191
	102,475
After-tax cash flow	$ 42,677

Table 12.8 Summary of Investor Return

Year	Sum Invested	Cash Flows	Tax Liability	Due at Reversion	Yearly Amounts
0	$27,000				$(27,000)
1		$ 15,830	$ 789		16,619
2		147	1,091		1,238
3		36	1,401		1,437
4		(80)	1,721		1,642
5		(200)	2,051		1,851
6		(326)	2,391		2,065
7		(457)	2,704		2,284
8		(593)	3,101		2,507
9		(736)	3,472		2,736
10		(885)	3,854	$42,677	45,646
Totals		$12,736	$22,611		$51,024

IRR = 19.9%

NPV_{15} = $5,823

Summary

Tax credits of 10 percent on the restoration of old buildings and 20 percent on the restoration of historic buildings significantly enhances the return on real estate investment projects, with certain limitations. The tax credit applies directly to tax liability arising from ordinary earned income, to a maximum of $8,333, depending on tax bracket. The tax credit may be applied against tax liability from passive income without limit in a given year, subject to the provisions of the Alternative Minimum Tax. Unused tax credits may be carried forward.

These provisions constitute significant incentives for investors to combine an old or historic building renovation with a conventional real estate investment project.

Chapter 13

Mini-Storage

Mini-storage facilities (also called mini-warehouses) are a specialized type of real estate investment that has proven very popular—and very successful—in recent years. From the consumer's point of view, a mini-warehouse provides a convenience. In an increasingly affluent and materialistic society, temporary or permanent storage of personal property can become a real problem. Demand for mini-storage space may also arise from small businesses that are conducted from personal residences or have outgrown their present facilities.

From an investor's point of view, mini-warehouses provide an attractive income potential, have low capital requirements, are relatively easy to manage, tend to be inflation-proof, and provide an excellent mechanism for holding land that may later be developed for residential, commercial, or industrial purposes.

The attractive income potential arises from the low cost of construction. Mini-warehouses are typically cinder blocks covered by a roof sitting on a concrete slab. Standard improvements include lights and a door. Mini-warehouses may also provide security in the form of a fence and guards. Cost of construction would typically run $15–20 per square foot. Typical prices to lessees for mini-warehouse storage on a monthly basis are $1 and up per square foot, depending on the level of security provided. Because maintenance and management costs are low, the underlying fundamentals of this investment are quite attractive.

One by-product of such an obviously attractive investment is a rush of capital into this business. In many urban areas, the market has been flooded with such facilities, resulting in high vacancy rates and falling prices.

The tendency for this market to be overbuilt makes location particularly important. The service provided by a mini-storage facility is convenience. A convenient location that cannot be readily duplicated by competitors provides a barrier against competition.

153

A desirable location would be defined in terms of its convenience and its competition (both present and potential). Convenience requires the close proximity of a large population that would create a demand for this type of service. Ease of access to the facility would also be required. A high-visibility location may be important to stimulating demand.

The present state of the market in a particular area can be readily assessed by a survey of existing facilities. If every existing mini-storage facility in an area has a waiting list, the market can probably bear more of this type of facility. As barriers to entry in this industry are low, investors should take care to assess the potential of others to enter the market.

General Investment Characteristics

Strengths

Cash Flow Characteristics. Mini-storage as an investment offers excellent cash flow characteristics due to its low variable costs and relatively low cost of construction. It would not be unusual for this type of facility to have a total fixed cost in its rentable space of $15 per square foot which consumers are eager to rent for $1 per square foot per month. This means investors can recapture the initial capital in 15 months, or significantly less if the project is leveraged.

Ease of Management. Because the space rented is not being used for residential purposes, continuing service is strictly a matter of whether the tenant pays (subject to whatever contractual provisions are specified). In addition, investors do not have to worry about such items as broken plumbing and furnaces that do not work.

Potential Appreciation. Many investors have found mini-storage an excellent vehicle to hold property for long-term appreciation. This type of land use is not capital-intensive, and with its good cash flow characteristics makes it an excellent device for waiting for shifts in land use patterns to make the property more valuable.

Inflation Protection. This type of investment protects investors doubly against the ravages of inflation. First, most costs are fixed. Second, leases for storage space are typically on a month-to-month basis, which means that rents can be easily raised in the face of general inflation.

Weaknesses

Scarcity of Good Locations. Because this type of project provides customers with convenience, location is quite important. Desirable locations may be difficult to find at reasonable prices. This type of investment cannot compete with more intensive uses of land (such as apartments and commercial facilities) because the cost of land does not matter as much in the total cost structure of an apartment or commercial facility. Keeping total fixed costs low is necessary for success with a mini-storage facility.

Excess Supply Conditions. Because of the good fundamentals of mini-storage as an investment, the market tends to be overbuilt. Overbuilding results in high vacancy rates and falling rents. Selecting a superior location is the only protection against this occurrence.

Insurance. Liability and property hazard insurance can become prohibitively expensive for this type of activity. Careful site selection and properly drawn leases minimize this problem.

Tax Considerations
Since mini-storage facilities are not particularly expensive to build, the potential for depreciation is low. However, considering the total investment, if the cost of land is low relative to that of the buildings, the investment may still yield some tax shelter and consequent tax savings. Mini-storage facilities are depreciable over a 31.5-year period.

When investors finance these projects, no interest expense can be charged against income. To the extent the project is leveraged, interest expense is deductible from revenues. This aspect of the project is particularly important if the mini-storage facilities are part of a strategy to hold raw land.

Case Study

Acquisition Phase. Suppose an investor buys two acres of land along a major highway on the urban fringe for $25,000. Eighty mini-warehouses are constructed for a total of 8,000 square feet at a cost of $17.50 per square foot (for a total of $140,000). A fence is constructed around the perimeter of the property at a cost of $25,000. The investor finances the project with $60,000 of her or his own capital and borrows the remaining

Table 13.1 Sources and Uses of Funds

Sources of funds	
Debt	$130,000
Equity	60,000
Total sources	$190,000
Uses of funds	
Land acquisition	$ 25,000
Building	140,000
Fence	25,000
Total uses	$190,000

$130,000 from a bank. The loan is for 15 years at 12 percent (see Table 13.1).

Holding Phase. Construction is completed in three months. The investor immediately rents 2,000 square feet at $1 per square foot. Three months later, the investor rents another 2,000 square foot at $1 per square foot. Six months after beginning the project, the investor rents another 2,000 square feet at $1 per square foot. Occupancy continues at this level for the first year. During the second and succeeding years, the investor leases 90 percent of the space. Rents the second year average $1.15 per square foot, and they rise 6 percent per year in subsequent years.

Property taxes, insurance, maintenance, and guard services cost $20,000 the first year and 25 percent of gross revenue thereafter. (Tables 13.2 and 13.3 present the results of these activities.)

The relatively small depreciation expense noted in Tables 13.2 and 13.3 results in little difference between the cash flow and income received in any given year. The loss during the first year reflects the low initial occupancy rate and signifies the critical impact of the utilization rate on the project's success. Subsequent profitable operations reflect continuing good demand characteristics for the service provided.

Disposal Phase. The investor holds the property for 10 years and then sells it to a developer for commercial purposes for $132,000 (from which the seller nets $120,000). This results in a gain on sale of $49,315 and tax liability of $13,808 for a net after-tax cash flow of $104,053. (Refer to Tables 13.4, 13.5, and 13.6 for these calculations.)

Table 13.2 Mini-Storage Income Statement

Year	1	2	3	4	5
Rental income	$36,000	$86,400	$91,584	$97,079	$102,904
Operating ex:					
Direct costs	20,000	21,600	22,896	24,270	25,726
Depr	3,795	5,280	5,280	5,280	5,280
Interest	15,422	15,004	14,532	14,001	13,402
Profit (loss)	($3,217)	$44,516	$48,876	$53,528	$58,496
Taxes	($901)	$12,464	$13,685	$14,988	$16,379

Year	6	7	8	9	10
Rental income	$109,078	$115,623	$122,560	$129,914	$137,708
Operating ex:					
Direct costs	27,270	28,906	30,640	32,478	34,427
Depr	5,280	5,280	5,280	5,280	5,280
Interest	12,727	11,967	11,110	10,144	9,057
Profit (loss)	$63,802	$69,470	$75,530	$82,011	$88,944
Taxes	$17,864	$19,452	$21,148	$22,963	$24,904

Table 13.3 Cash Flow Statement Mini-Storage

Year	1	2	3	4	5
Rental income	$36,000	$86,400	$91,584	$97,079	$102,904
Operating ex:					
Taxes	20,000	21,600	22,896	24,270	25,726
Debt service	18,723	18,723	18,723	18,723	18,723
Cash flow	($2,723)	$46,077	$49,965	$54,086	$58,455

Table 13.3 (continued)

Year	6	7	8	9	10
Rental income	$109,078	$115,623	$122,560	$129,914	$137,708
Operating ex:					
Taxes	27,270	28,906	30,640	32,478	34,427
Debt service	18,723	18,723	18,723	18,723	18,723
Cash flow	$63,086	$67,994	$73,197	$78,712	$84,558

Table 13.4 Basis Calculation

Cost of property	$190,000
Less depreciation	51,000
Adjusted basis	$138,685

Table 13.5 Tax Schedule

Net sales	$188,000
Adjusted basis	138,685
Gain on sale	$ 49,315
Tax liability (28% of gain)	13,808
After-tax gain	$ 35,507

Table 13.6 Net After-Tax Cash Flow

Selling price	$200,000
Less:	
Selling commission	12,000
Mortgage balance	70,139
Taxes	13,808
Net cash flow	$104,053

The project ultimately earns a spectacular IRR of 44.6 percent and a NPV at 21 percent of $142,087. This high return was a function of the profitability of operations rather than appreciation in the value of the land (see Table 13.7).

Table 13.7 Evaluation of Return

Year	Cash Flow	After-Tax Reversion	Taxes	Total
–0				$(60,000)
1	$(2,723)		$ (901)	(1,822)
2	46,077		12,464	33,613
–3	49.965		13,685	36,280
4	54,086		14,988	39,098
5	58,455		16,379	42,076
6	63,086		17,864	45,221
7	67,994		19,452	48,542
8	73,197		21,148	52,049
9	78,712		22,963	55,749
10	84,558	$104,053	24,904	163,707
	$573,407		$162,948	$454,512

IRR = 44.6%
NPV_{21} = $142,087

Summary

Mini-storage facilities constitute exceptionally attractive investments for aggressive investors. Mini-storage facilities require little capital, have small variable costs, and, if properly located, will experience increasing demand. The net result of these circumstances is likely to be very strong income and cash-flow characteristics. An additional advantage of mini-storage facilities is that they provide an excellent means to hold land for future appreciation.

Investors must be wary of the market being saturated by excess competition. This situation could quickly drive rates or occupancy level to negative profitability.

Chapter 14

Shopping Centers

Shopping centers often provide real estate investors with substantial opportunities for above average return on their investment. Successfully investing in shopping centers requires a high level of skill and good judgement. Few kinds of real estate investing require so much from the investor. As in other areas of real estate, risk and reward go hand-in-hand.

Shopping centers come in a variety of sizes and types. Investors of modest means may develop or purchase a small center directly, or they may indirectly participate in the largest shopping centers through master limited partnerships (MLPs) or real estate investment trusts (REITs).

Although shopping center investments may differ widely in form and type, the elements that make the investment profitable are the same.

Indirect Investment

Indirect investment in a shopping center generally involves participating in some form of investment syndicate. Many large regional shopping centers are owned by MLPs or REITs.

MLPs and REITs, if they are actively traded on one of the major or over-the-counter markets, provide investors with a significant degree of liquidity. Active markets also provide investors with access to information about the value of their shares or units.

Limited partnership units can be purchased through public or private offerings. A public offering of a limited partnership requires that investors receive a prospectus describing the offering in great detail. Public limited offerings allow an investment of as little as $1,000. Private offerings to "sophisticated" investors are made through the use of a private placement memorandum. This type of investment normally requires much larger amounts of capital.

The desirability of this type of investment depends largely on the projected earnings of the shopping center under consideration. Tax advantages tend to be minimal because so much of the value of large shopping centers is tied up in nondepreciable land rather than depreciable buildings.

Important questions to consider in evaluating shopping center investment opportunities through MLPs or REITS would include these: Is the shopping center anchored by strong national tenants? Will the shopping center dominate its trading area? Does the market (or will the market) suffer from debilitating competition? Does management use strong triple-net leases, in which the tenant bears the cost of taxes, insurance, and common area maintainence that escalate rents as sales volume rises? Is the mix of tenants appropriate for the market to be served?

Direct Investment

Many types of smaller shopping center opportunities do not require great wealth to exploit. Certainly, shopping center development is not for everyone. However, for aggressive investors who already have successful experience in apartments or office buildings, shopping center opportunities may offer exceptionally high returns.

The potential returns in this area are so high because the risks are so great. A drive through almost any urban area reveals smaller shopping centers in obviously decrepit condition with unleased space. These failed investments serve as grim reminders that even the best laid plans sometimes go awry.

Types of Shopping Centers

Strip Shopping Centers. Two to five small, independent stores clustered on a heavily travelled road. The majority of business derives from the passing traffic. Land area is normally small—one-half to one acre.

Neighborhood Shopping Centers. Two to five small, independent stores serving a local market of between 5,000 and 10,000. Center location must have good access and prominence to the neighborhood served.

Community Shopping Centers. Two to eight small stores anchored by a local or regional chain store that builds traffic. This type of center typically serves a market with population between 20,000 and 40,000. The community shopping center must be on a major traffic artery and have high visibility to the community served.

Inner City Shopping Centers. Two to five small, independent businesses located on one or two floors of a large building in a densely-populated urban area. A center located in a residential area functions to service the neighborhood. A center located in an area of office buildings and other commercial enterprises meets the needs of its transient population.

Requirements for Success

When shopping centers are successful, investors are rewarded with a constant stream of revenue that provides an excellent return on the initial investment. Where the center shows evidence of stability or steady growth in earnings, the center may be readily sold to other investors, allowing the original investors to recoup both their initial investment and a handsome profit.

A shopping center is successful when its tenants are successful. For this to happen, the center must be located so that it can serve the intended market, and that market must be large enough to support the tenant stores. The prime danger is that the market may be too thin as a result of present or future competition. The center's tenants must provide appropriate goods and services to the intended market. The tenants must be enterprises that are adequately capitalized and managed.

Successful small shopping center investors find an appropriate location, put together financing for the project, coordinate the design and construction of the center, and secure the right tenants. This task requires determination and skill. It is not a task to be undertaken by the faint-hearted.

Finding a Match Between Location and Tenants

Assessing Location

The key factor in any real estate investment is location. It is especially important for shopping centers. The viability of any shopping center depends on the support the market can be expected to give prospective tenants. Therefore, a key first step in assessing a location is to develop an estimate of market size and boundaries.

Aerial photographs of a potential location are a good first step in assessing market size and boundaries. These are normally available from city, county, or state planning agencies. An examination of this map will suggest trading area boundaries. Other existing, and potential, shopping center sites may also be determined from this map.

Investors can examine census tract data (available in larger local libraries) to estimate the size, age, and income characteristics of the population in the indicated market area. Combined with traffic count data (available from the local highway department), this data suggests what kind of tenants would do well at the potential site.

Setting Rent Levels

Investors should consider the profit potential of various rent structures before approaching potential tenants. Different tenants will have different preferences for space, layout, and building appearance. It is very difficult to solicit desirable tenants without some specifics, which means that investors will have to spend some funds before even approaching tenants.

The first step in this process of examining a project's revenues and expenses to see whether the project will be viable would be to survey the price of comparable commercial space in the area. If comparable space has an annual lease rate of $12–18 per square foot, it would not be unreasonable to assume the proprosed project could bring $15 per square foot.

If a 10,000-square foot project is planned, with land costs of $5 per square foot, and discussions with local builders suggest that building costs will be $40 per square foot, then a total investment of $450,000 will be required. The ratio of total investment to gross rents will be 3-to-1 at a net rental of $15 per square foot. This could be considered an attractive ratio and would probably justify the expense and effort to find tenants willing to make a commitment to the proposed shopping center.

Selecting Lease Characteristics

In the shopping center business, leases are life. Commercial tenants normally want a long lease if they are going to spend time and money building up a location. This is good, except that investors do not want to be in a situation where their revenues are fixed and their expenses are not. The lease spells out who pays what. The following general types of leases are used in shopping centers (investors should have a lawyer draw up specific leases):

Gross Lease. The landlord pays all expenses except remodeling costs and nonstructural maintenance costs in the tenant area. The tenant pays a fixed rent for the life of the lease.

Net Lease. Like a gross lease, except the tenant is responsible for a proportionate share of property taxes.

Double Net Lease. Like a net lease, except the tenant pays a proportionate share of insurance expense.

Triple Net Lease. Like a double net lease, except the tenant pays a proportionate share of building maintenance (including common area) expenses.

Triple Net Lease with Percentage. Like a triple net lease, except the tenant pays a minimum amount of rent plus some percentage of gross sales over some specified level of sales.

Triple Net Lease with Ups. Like a triple net lease, except the rent is indexed to some measure of inflation (such as the Consumer Price Index) for the life of the lease.

From the investors' point of view, the triple net lease with percentage or ups is the most desirable. Whether a commercial tenant will agree to such terms depends on its estimate of the desirability of the location. Almost all leases for prime locations utilize triple net leases with percentage and ups.

Finding Financing

Commercial banks and other financial institutions are often willing to provide capital for small shopping centers, under certain conditions. The most important condition is that the investor have signed leases from strong tenants. Bankers generally consider building a shopping center without good tenants in hand as speculative behavior and want no part of it unless the loan is well secured by other assets. Additional factors affecting the willingness of banks to consider this kind of loan include the general completeness and professionalism of the plan.

Even with strong tenants committed to the project, bankers normally want an exposed mortgage. An *exposed mortgage* is made on a property for which a significant portion of the capital is invested by the borrower.

A bank may require a *participation mortgage* as a condition for making the loan. This allows the bank to take some portion of the cash flow as part of the price of the loan. Compared to projects with similar degrees of risk, a project with a participation mortgage carries a lower rate of interest.

General Investment Characteristics

Strengths

High Returns. The underlying economics of a fully-leased shopping center yield an excellent return on investment. A competitive rent structure with normal building and development costs yields a return superior to most other investment opportunities.

Protection from Inflation. The use of triple net leases with percentage not only provides investors with a complete inflation hedge, it also builds in increasing profitability.

Opportunity to Improve Profitability. Leases, while long term, do not last forever. At some point they can be renegotiated. A successful center can use this opportunity to further increase profits.

Weaknesses

Up-Front Costs. Successfully developing a small shopping center requires an up-front commitment of capital and effort.

Exposure to Risk from General Economic Decline. Deterioration in national or regional economic conditions (increasing unemployment, declining personal income) can lead to a decline in the viability of a tenant's business. This situation may result in a significant decrease in rental income where the leases are on a percentage basis. Where leases are not thoroughly collateralized, it is difficult to collect any rent at all from a failing tenant.

Exposure to Risk from Market Saturation. A competing small shopping center may invade the market and cause a deterioration of tenant sales or the failure of tenant businesses.

A larger shopping center may invade the trading area as a result of some change in the transportation system, a change in consumer shopping patterns, or more aggressive marketing on the part of that shopping center. This could cause lost sales to tenants or failure of tenant businesses.

Exposure to Risk from Increasing Interest Rates. A runup in interest rates and an increase in the scarcity of money generally has an adverse impact on the demand for commercial retail space. This occurs because retailers generally use float to finance some or all of their inventories. *Float* arises from the time between when a retailer receives merchandise and when it is paid for. When the availability of float diminishes or float becomes more expensive, they cut back or at least are unable to expand their inventories. This results in reduced demand for retail space.

Risk from Tenant Failure. Tenants may fail just because they are poorly managed or suffer from some unique mishap. This may result in lost rents and unrented space.

Capital Availability. The availability of capital for this type of enterprise does not allow as much leverage as is available for other types of real estate investment. Investors may have to secure the loan by pledging other assets or signing personally. Capital may be available only in the form of a participatory loan.

Summary of Weaknesses

With this type of investment, fixed costs are relatively high and revenues variable as a result of many factors, some of which are controllable and some of which are not. This cost–revenue structure simultaneously gives small shopping centers their high potential for profit or loss.

Tax Considerations

Most of the land for a small shopping center is used for parking. The land itself is expensive relative to total building costs, since location is of such importance. These factors mean that only a small portion of the total investment is depreciable, compared with other real estate investments. Thus, substantial depreciation will not be available to shield revenues from taxes.

Losses may be applied against ordinary income to a maximum of $25,000, depending on the investor's tax bracket, for a maximum tax saving of $8,333. Passive losses may be applied against passive income without limit.

Case Study

Acquisition Phase. Suppose an investor purchases a six-month option on two adjacent closed gas stations and a vacant lot, for a total area of 1.75 acres. The options cost $5,000, and the properties may be purchased for a total of $90,000. During the six-month period the investor analyzes the market; consults with architects, builders, lawyers, bankers; and solicits tenants. Direct costs associated with these activities are $5,000.

As a result of these activities, the investor decides that the optimal use of this property is as a neighborhood shopping center. An appropriate building is constructed with 8,000 square feet of gross leasing area and no common area. Commitment is gained from four prospective tenants.

The largest tenant is a local hardware store chain for 3,000 square feet at an annual rate of $10 per square foot. The lease is triple net for ten years with two five-year options. There is an ups for three percent per year.

An independent fast food store leases 2,000 square feet at an annual rate of $12 per square foot. The lease is triple net with a percentage--two percent of gross sales above $15,000 per month. The lease is for ten years with two five-year options.

An independent pet store leases 2,000 square feet for an annual rate of $9 per square foot. The lease is triple net for five years with no options and no percentage or ups.

An independent jewelry store leases 1,000 square feet at an annual rate of $15 per square foot. The lease is triple net with a five-percent ups. The lease is for ten years with two five-year options.

The cost of the building is $40 per square foot for a total of $320,000.

A bank is found that is willing to lend the investor $300,000 at 12 percent plus 5 percent of gross revenues. The loan is amortized at a 30-year rate but balloons in ten years. As Table 14.1 shows, this requires the investor to put up personal capital of $120,000.

Table 14.1 Investment Data

Capital required	
Cost of land	$ 90,000
Building	320,000
Related fee	5,000
Closing costs	5,000
Total capital required:	$420,000
Sources of capital	
Mortgage (12% for 30 years)	$300,000
Investor's capital	120,000
Total capital provided:	$420,000

Holding Phase. The fast food store runs into trouble after six months and ceases to pay rent. It takes another six months to evict this business and replace it. It is replaced by a national fast food chain with a triple net lease for ten years with two five-year options, rent of $6 per square foot, and ups at 10 percent annually.

The pet store is both badly managed and undercapitalized. It pays one month's rent then ceases to pay rent. It takes the entire first year to evict the pet store and find another tenant. A regional bookstore chain signs a triple net lease for ten years with two five-year options, rent of $10 per square foot, and 5 percent ups annually.

Table 14.2 depicts the impact of these changes on the investor's income. Note the significant drop of income in year one because the tenants failed to pay rent. The robust performance of income over the ten-year period reflects both the stability in tenant occupancy and the operation of the ups.

Table 14.2 Income Statement—Shopping Center Project

Year	1	2	3	4	5
Rental income:					
Hardware store	$30,000	$30,900	$31,827	$32,782	$33,765
Fast food	12,000				
Food chain		6,000	13,200	14,520	15,972
Pet store	1,500				
Book store		20,000	21,000	22,050	23,153
Jewelry store	15,000	15,750	16,538	17,364	18,233
Total rent due	$58,500	$72,650	$82,565	$86,716	$91,122
Less:					
Operating ex:					
Depreciation	9,750	10,400	10,400	10,400	10,400
Interest expense	38,866	39,436	39,776	39,808	39,831
Profit (loss)	$9,884	$22,815	$32,388	$36,508	$40,891
Taxes due (28%)	$2,768	$6,388	$9,069	$10,222	$11,450

Table 14.2 (continued)

Year	6	7	8	9	10
Rental income:					
Hardware store	$34,778	$35,822	$36,896	$38,003	$39,143
Fast food					
Food chain	17,569	19,326	21,259	23,385	25,723
Pet store					
Book store	24,310	25,526	26,802	28,142	29,549
Jewelry store	19,144	20,101	21,107	22,162	23,270
Total rent due	$95,802	$100,775	$106,063	$111,692	$117,685
Less:					
Operating ex:					
Depreciation	10,400	10,400	10,400	10,400	10,400
Interest expense	39,842	39,840	39,822	39,785	39,725
Profit (loss)	$45,560	$50,535	$55,841	$61,507	$67,560
Taxes due (28%)	$12,757	$14,150	$15,636	$17,222	$18,917

Table 14.3 shows cash flow rising from $18,545 in year one to $74,771 in year ten. In all years, cash flow exceeds income, although the spread narrows as more of the building loan is paid off.

Table 14.3 Cash Flow Statement—Shopping Center Project

Year	1	2	3	4	5
Rental income:					
Hardware store	$30,000	$30,900	$31,827	$32,782	$33,765
Fast food	12,000				
Food chain		6,000	13,200	14,520	15,972
Pet store	1,500				
Book store		20,000	21,000	22,050	23,153
Jewelry store	15,000	15,750	16,538	17,364	18,233
Total rent due	$58,500	$72,650	$82,565	$86,716	$91,122
Less:					
Debt service	39,955	40,663	41,158	41,366	41,586
Cash flow	$18,545	$31,988	$41,406	$45,350	$49,536

Table 14.3 (continued)

Year	6	7	8	9	10
Rental income:					
Hardware store	$34,778	$35,822	$36,896	$38,003	$39,143
Fast food					
Food chain	17,569	19,326	21,259	23,385	25,723
Pet store					
Book store	24,310	25,526	26,802	28,142	29,549
Jewelry store	19,144	20,101	21,107	22,162	23,270
Total rent due	$95,802	$100,775	$106,063	$111,692	$117,685
Less:					
Debt service	41,820	42,069	42,333	42,615	42,914
Cash flow	$53,982	$58,706	$63,730	$69,077	$74,771

Disposal Phase. At the end of ten years, the project yields $74,771 net income. As a result of the demonstrated stability of tenants and rent revenues, the investor is able to sell the small shopping center for more than nine times earnings, $706,112. To determinine the tax liability arising from the sale, the investor calculates the basis as in Table 14.4.

Table 14.4 Basis Calculation

Acquisition costs	$420,000
Less:	
Accumulated depreciation	103,350
Adjusted basis	$316,650

Table 14.5 shows that the resultant tax liability is $97,187, which provides an after-tax cash flow of $286,304 in year ten (see Table 14.6).

Table 14.5 Tax Liability Analysis

Net sale price		$663,745
Less:		
Adjusted basis		316,650
Gain on sale		$347,095
Tax liability (28% of gain)	$97,187	

Table 14.6 After-Tax Cash Flow

Selling price		$706,112
Less:		
Selling expenses (6%)	42,367	
Mortgage balance	280,254	
Tax liability	97,187	
		$419,808
After-tax cash flow		$286,304

Using a risk-adjusted discount rate of 21 percent on the cash flow over the ten years yields a net present value of $55,371. The corresponding internal rate of return yields the investor a sparkling 29.2-percent annual return on the investment of $120,000. Table 14.7 presents the summary of investor returns.

Summary

Successful direct investing in shopping centers requires a high degree of business judgement and management skill. Shopping centers are successful only if their tenants are successful. The successful investor in a shopping center not only needs to select a location, obtain financing, and construct an appropriate building, but must also select a mix of tenants whose individual services and products will complement one another sufficiently to build a critical mass in the market served.

The rewards for this business acumen can be outstanding. Less accurate judgement is often punished by the market. Even when excellent decisions are made, success is not guaranteed. Forces beyond the investor's control can devastate the market and place the project in jeopardy.

The aggressive, shrewd investor can find profitable opportunities in this market. All others tread at their own peril.

Table 14.7 Summary of Investor Return

Year	Sum Invested	Cash Flows	Tax Liability	Due at Reversion	Yearly Amounts
0	$120,000				$(120,000)
1		$ 18,545	$ 2,768		15,777
2		31,988	6,388		25,599
3		41,406	9,069		32,338
4		45,350	10,222		35,128
5		49,536	11,450		38,087
6		53,982	12,757		41,225
7		58,706	14,150		44,556
8		63,730	15,636		48,095
9		69,077	17,222		51,855
10		74,771	18,917	$286,304	342,159
Totals		$507,091	$118,577		$674,819

IRR = 29.2%
NPV_{21} = $55,371

Chapter 15

Office Buildings

Few real estate investments offer more opportunities, and risks, than office buildings. A successful office building project can offer exceptionally high returns. A well-located building with good physical attributes and desirable amenities can attract solid, prestigious tenants almost without regard to price if there is a shortage of desirable office space. However, even good buildings will go vacant if they come into the market at a time when there is a glut of office space. Vacant office space in Houston exceeded fifty percent throughout the mid 1980s.

The market for office space offers investors a wide array of options. Office buildings range from those requiring very modest capital to the most expensive properties in the city. Such diversity represents opportunity to the aggressive investor.

Generalizations are difficult to make in the face of such a differentiated market. Substantial profits can be made by recognizing value where others do not see it. This recognition requires an understanding of the office building market and how it works.

Demand

Location

The demand for space in a particular office building depends on a number of factors. Location is of prime importance, in several different senses.

Location is important in terms of prestige. If you are an investment banker in New York City, you must be on Wall Street. Every town has its Wall Street.

Location is important in terms of access to market or shared resources: Lawyers like to be prominently located near the courthouse; physicians near the hospital. Banks, insurance companies, mutual funds, stockbrokers are happiest located close together in the financial district. Organizations employing similar types of people tend to cluster together.

Locations are subject to trends in fashion. Such trends are difficult to forecast. One location's prestige endures over time. Other locations fall in and out of fashion in a manner reminiscent of the fashion cycle in women's apparel.

Location is important in terms of visibility. A building's physical prominence, style, and distinguishing characteristics are important. Equally important are the similar attributes of the other nearby buildings.

Location is also important in terms of access to transportation. Ease of access to major highways, railroads, public transportation and airports may be required by prospective tenants. Access to public services such as the post office or government agencies may be important.

The atmosphere of a particular location may prove an asset or a liability. The ambience of the neighborhood, the physical surroundings of the buildings, and the presence or absence of public amenities all play a role in determining the desirability of a particular office location.

Building Characteristics

The demand for office space may be highly specialized. Lawyers need conference rooms, dentists need lots of plumbing, some companies need large open spaces, and others need small, fixed offices. Office space often needs to be designed or remodeled to suit the needs of an individual tenant.

Amenities are often critical to the desirability of a particular office. The capacity of the heating and cooling systems, the adequacy of the elevator system, the availability of parking, the quality of maintenance and cleaning services, the security system, and the presence of in-building shops all strongly influence the decision to locate or remain in a particular building.

Regional Factors

The demand for office space in a particular region may be influenced by the area's rate of economic growth. Existing industries may be expanding or contracting. New industries may be coming in or old industries leaving. New business may be forming at a more or less rapid rate. Local businesses may be consolidating outlying operations. Technological changes, such as the widespread use of computer-based information systems, may require different types of office layouts and utilities.

As the demand for office space is not particularly sensitive to price, small shifts in the general demand for office space may have a disproportionate impact on the price of office space. Changes in the regional demand for office building space can quickly bring feast or famine for office building owners.

Supply

As the demand for office space presses on the supply of office space in a particular area, price does not move until capacity is approached. At that point, price moves very rapidly, signalling the market for an increase in supply. An increase in the supply of office space will be two to five years coming. During that time, office space rents rise higher and higher, prompting frenzied supply activity. The result in seven years is excess office space capacity and plummeting office rents that cannot cure high vacancy rates. Successful real estate investing is as much a matter of timing as anything else.

Form of Ownership

For most investors, direct ownership of skyscrapers in the downtown business district is not practical. This is the province of insurance companies and the super-rich. However, indirect ownership is possible through MLPs and REITs. Projects with good buildings in desirable locations that are entering the market during the right phase of the cycle can do very well.

A variety of direct ownership forms are possible for many investors. Within the general market for office space are many specialized niches that the modest investor may reasonably undertake. For example, converting a three-story apartment building near a large hospital to doctors' offices may prove quite attractive. Converting a decrepit motel adjacent to the central business district to offices for small professionals accountants, lawyers, architects, financial services, real estate agents, and insurance agents who need the location but can't afford the price of the prestigious high-rises may prove a worthwhile endeavor.

A key factor in the success of an office building is securing a good anchor tenant. For this reason, a small firm or professional partnership often develops and occupies its own office building, thus becoming its own anchor tenant. The firm itself can own the building or, in order to take advantage of tax considerations, the principals may form a limited partnership to own the building.

Financial Attractiveness

In the absence of an excess supply of office space, the prevailing rent structure generally offers investors handsome returns—assuming that the property under consideration has no trouble attracting and holding desirable tenants. Abstracting from land costs which can be generally handled by a sale and leaseback arrangement to minimize capital expenditures, low-rise office space costs $40–60 per square foot and rents for $1.50–3.00 per square foot per month in many good urban locations. This mean a 10,000-square-foot building costs about $500,000 and brings in gross rents of approximately $270,000 annually. Even if expenses run 40 percent of gross rents, $162,000 is clearly going to more than cover the cost of capital.

Finding Financing

Banks and other financial institutions are often eager to lend to investors in office buildings under certain conditions. Because the big risk in this type of investment is that tenants may be difficult to secure, banks and other financial institutions generally require investors to have contractual commitments from solid companies for the office space to be built. This may be difficult to do, since the lead time in office building construction is so long. A variation of this requirement constructs the mortgage so that capital is advanced in portions as leases are obtained.

In the absence of secured, financially-solid leases, financing is hard to come by. Where capital is available for office buildings, banks generally want loans collateralized by more than the building to be constructed. They also want to participate in the gross revenue stream produced by the property. During the periods of tight money in the late 1970s and early 1980s, some banks demanded (and got!) 50-percent participation in gross revenues.

Leases

Leases generally run five to ten years, although longer leases are not uncommon. Leases are generally not net of taxes and insurance. The owner is often protected from inflationary pressures by some ups in the rent tied to an inflation index such as the Consumer Price Index.

Building owners are often responsible for interior alteration to suit the tenant's requirements. Alterations can be quite expensive, running up to 30 percent of the cost of construction. Building owners generally assume the responsibility for providing maintenance, cleaning services, and security. These costs usually run between 25 and 40 percent of gross rents, depending on the quality of service desired.

General Investment Characteristics

Strengths

High Returns. The cost of developing office space relative to the rent obtainable is quite favorable under normal conditions. Profits may be further enhanced by periodic market shortages of office space. Assuming that locational and amenity requirements are met, price is often not a deciding factor in the decision to rent a particular office.

Ease of Management. Dealing with businesses avoids many of the headaches associated with residential rentals. The services provided by building owners are generally farmed out to independent contractors.

Stability of Rents. Long-term leases in combination with financially-stable tenants reduce problems arising from turnover and nonpayment.

Capital Availability. Where leases are properly secured, financing is readily forthcoming.

Weaknesses

High Risk. The market is inherently unstable because of the periodic conditions of oversupply. If economic uncertainties or downturns result in a fall in demand, vacancies are not easily curable. Cash flow under these circumstances may be negative, causing the property to lose liquidity.

Capital Availability. Without secured leases in hand, capital financing is both very difficult to get and quite expensive.

Lead Times. The time between the formation of the idea to develop a property and the actual installation of tenants is at least two to three years. During this time, considerable expense is incurred on construction, planning, and associated activities.

Tax Considerations

Office buildings generate tax shelter through the depreciation of building costs (less land) over a 31.5-year period. Appreciation in the value of the building is taxed at the same rates as ordinary income. The implications of tax considerations on office building investment are specified in the case study that follows. (See Chapter 4 for a fuller discussion of the general tax treatment of real estate investments.)

Case Study

Acquisition Stage. Suppose an investor in the 28-percent tax bracket develops an office building in the following manner. The investor purchases for $60,000 an old railway station adjacent to the town's central business district. A zoning change is secured and an architect is engaged to develop plans for an office building of 12,000 square feet at a cost of $50 per square foot, for a total cost of $600,000. These activities cost $5,000. The investor advances the necessary capital directly.

The investor solicits tenants and secures a lease with a major blue-chip overnight delivery service. The lease is for ten years with two five-year options for 6,000 square feet at $1.35 per square foot per month with an annual 5-percent up. The lease is scheduled to take effect with the completion of the building two years hence.

Six months prior to the completion of the building, the investor secures a lease from a national fast food franchiser for 4,000 square feet of office space. The lease is for ten years with one five-year option at a monthly rate of $2.00 per square foot per month and an annual 8-percent up. At this time the investor secures two additional tenants for the remaining 2,000 square feet. An urban planning firm takes 1,000 square feet on an annual lease of $2.50 per square foot per month with no up. A law firm takes the remaining 1,000 square feet for five years at $2.25 per square foot per month with 6-percent up. Necessary interior modifications for the four clients total $120,000.

On the strength of these leases, the investor negotiates a $600,000 mortgage from an insurance company on the building. The mortgage is for 20 years at 10 percent plus 5 percent of gross revenues (see Table 15.1).

Table 15.1 Sources and Uses of Funds

Sources of funds

Debt	$600,000
Equity	120,000
Total sources	$720,000

Uses of funds

Land acquisition	$ 60,000
Building	620,000
Fees	5,000
Closing costs	35,000
Total uses	$720,000

Holding Phase. Annual taxes on the property are $6,000 and rise 5 percent annually. Insurance, maintenance, cleaning services, and security run 30 percent of gross rent. After the first year, the urban planning firm signs a ten-year lease with a 3-percent up at $2.75 per square foot per month. After five years, the lawyer leaves. This space is vacant for six months and is then leased to an accountant at $2.75 with a 5-percent annual up.

Under these circumstances, the office building project shows a modest profit during the ten years of operation. Income rises from $17,097 in the first year to $109,611 in the tenth year. The escalation largely reflects the presence of stable tenants and ups in the leases. Table 15.2 shows the income statement for the project.

The substantial increases in cash flow depicted in Table 15.3 on page 187 reflects trends similar to those shown on the income statement. The cash flow starts higher but does not rise nearly as rapidly, due to the effect of principal replacing interest in the mortgage payment.

Disposal Phase. After ten years the investor sells the property to a developer who demolishes it to make way for a skyscraper. The property realizes $900,000 net of closing costs but not sales commissions. The tax liability arising from the sale of property would be calculated in the following manner. Table 15.4 on page 187 reveals the adjusted basis of the property (initial cost less depreciation) as $521,250. This yields a gain of $324,750 and, in the 28-percent bracket, a consequent tax liability of $90,930 for an after-tax return of $233,820. The net cash flow of $316,922 realized from the sale is larger by the amount of mortgage payments made toward equity (see Table 15.5 on page 188).

Table 15.2 Income Statement—Office Building Project

Year	1	2	3	4	5
Revenue from:					
Delivery service	$82,800	$86,940	$91,287	$95,851	$100,644
Fast food	72,000	77,760	83,981	90,699	97,955
Urban planning	24,000	24,000	24,000	30,000	30,900
Law firm	24,000	25,440	26,966	28,584	30,299
Accounting firm	0	0	0	0	0
Total rent	$202,800	$214,140	$226,234	$245,135	$259,799
Operating ex:					
Main/Insur	91,260	96,363	101,805	110,311	116,909
Taxes	6,000	6,300	6,615	6,946	7,293
Depr	18,750	20,000	20,000	20,000	20,000
Interest	69,693	69,826	68,677	68,353	67,685
Profit (loss)	$17,097	$21,651	$29,137	$39,526	$47,911
Taxes	$4,787	$6,062	$8,158	$11,067	$13,415

Year	6	7	8	9	10
Revenue from:					
Delivery service	$105,676	$110,960	$116,508	$122,333	$128,450
Fast food	105,792	114,255	123,395	133,267	143,928
Urban planning	31,827	32,782	33,765	34,778	35,822
Law firm	0	0	0	0	0
Accounting firm	13,500	35,700	37,485	39,359	41,327
Total rent	$256,795	$293,697	$311,154	$329,739	$349,527
Operating ex:					
Main/Insur	115,558	132,164	140,019	148,382	157,287
Taxes	7,658	8,041	8,443	8,865	9,308
Depr	20,000	20,000	20,000	20,000	20,000
Interest	65,986	66,121	65,104	63,946	62,629
Profit (loss)	$47,594	$67,372	$77,588	$88,545	$109,611
Taxes	$13,326	$18,864	$21,725	$24,793	$30,691

Table 15.3 Cash Flow Statement—Office Building Project

Year	1	2	3	4	5
Delivery service	$82,800	$86,940	$91,287	$95,851	$100,644
Fast food	72,000	77,760	83,981	90,699	97,955
Urban planning	24,000	24,000	24,000	30,000	30,900
Law firm	24,000	25,440	26,966	28,584	30,900
Accounting firm	0	0	0	0	0
Total	$202,800	$214,140	$226,234	$245,135	$259,799
Operating ex:					
Main/Insur	91,260	96,363	101,805	110,311	116,909
Taxes	6,000	6,300	6,615	6,946	7,293
Debt service	79,621	80,188	80,793	81,738	82,471
Cash flow	$25,919	$31,289	$37,021	$46,141	$53,125

Year	6	7	8	9	10
Delivery service	$105,676	$110,960	$116,508	$122,333	$128,450
Fast food	105,792	114,255	123,395	133,267	143,928
Urban planning	31,827	32,782	33,765	34,778	35,822
Law firm	0	0	0	0	0
Accounting firm	13,500	35,700	37,485	39,359	41,327
Total	$256,795	$293,697	$311,154	$329,738	$349,527
Operating ex:					
Main/Insur	115,558	132,164	140,019	148,382	157,287
Taxes	7,658	8,041	8,443	8,865	9,308
Debt service	82,321	84,166	85,039	85,968	86,957
Cash flow	$51,259	$69,327	$77,653	$86,523	$95,975

Table 15.4 After-Tax Cash Flow

Net sales	$846,000
Adjusted basis	521,250
Gain on sale	$324,750
Tax liability	90,930
After-tax return	$233,820

Table 15.5 Basis Calculation

Cost of property	$720,000
Less depreciation	198,750
Adjusted basis	$521,250
Selling price	$900,000
Less:	
Selling commission	54,000
Mortgage balance	438,148
Taxes	90,930
Net cash flow	$316,922

The profitability of the project can be evaluated in terms of net present value or internal rate of return. Table 15.6 presents these calculations. The absolute cash flow produced by the project is $618,265; when discounted at an annual rate of 21 percent, it yields a net present value of $68,120 for an internal rate of return of 30.7 percent. This rate of return on a project of this type may be considered normal in a healthy office space market.

Table 15.6 Investment Evaluation

Year	Cash Flow	After-Tax Reversion	Taxes	Total
0				$(120,000)
1	$25,919'		$ 4,787	21,132
2	31,28		6,062	25,227
3	37,021		8,158	28,863
4	46,141		11,067	35,074
5	53,125		13,415	39,710
6	51,259		13,326	37,932
7	69,327		18,864	50,463
8	77,653		21,725	55,928
9	86,523		24,793	61,731
10	$95,975	$316,922	30,691	382,206
	$574,231		$152,889	$618,265

IRR = 30.7%
NPV_{21} = $68,120

Summary

Investments in office buildings present investors with both substantial opportunities and risks. In the case study developed, the investor earned an annual return of 30.7 percent on a $120,000 investment over a ten-year period. It is entirely within the realm of possibility that this return could have been much higher had a periodic shortage of office space occurred when office space was being leased or the building sold.

In a similar fashion, had a periodic glut of office space occurred at these times, the investor would have faced a possible disaster. Under most conditions when supply is relatively fixed, small changes in demand can bring about dramatic changes in price. On those occasions when the market becomes overbuilt, prices fall and vacancy rates increase.

The office space market is fast-paced and volatile. For aggressive investors, it offers tremendous challenge and opportunity along with great risk.

Chapter 16

Industrial Properties

Industrial property real estate investments range from small to very large. Some industrial projects have very little risk; other industrial properties are highly speculative. Aggressive investors can find opportunities for profit in this market.

A Fortune 500 tenant willing to sign a long-term lease on a property built to suit will demand and receive a square-foot price that approaches the investor's cost. The low return corresponds to the low risk. An investment of this type is similar to buying an industrial bond.

At the other end of the spectrum, if an investor correctly anticipates local industrial growth patterns and develops a desirable property in advance of that need, a lease for such property can be secured that has a handsome return indeed. In the absence of competing locations and given the time necessary to build, an industrial firm would have little choice but to pay the asking price.

Investment in industrial real estate properties offers unique advantages and disadvantages. The large scale of investment required and the nature of risk in this area generally result in industrial property being developed by a syndicate in some form rather than by an individual. Properly structured, this form of investment may provide superior returns for the small or medium-sized investor.

Use-Specific Needs

Industrial property tends to be very use-specific. Different industries have substantially different requirements for the construction, layout, and facilities of their physical plants. Even within a particular industry, significant variation exists between the manufacturing processes of individual firms. Recent trends toward "focused factories" and rapid technological change have increased the need for flexibility and increased the dangers of obsolescence.

193

Because such significant differences exist among potential users of an industrial property, correctly anticipating the type of user is of critical importance to the investor. Perhaps the best way to minimize this problem is to negotiate a lease with a prime client prior to construction.

Investors may expect to encounter a variety of preferences. Windows are important for assembly or manufacturing operations but not desirable for warehouses. Level floors are necessary for assembly or manufacturing processes, but a food processor requires sloping floors with drainage. Some manufacturing operations require substantial venting or lighting; others do not. Labor-intensive operations require more washroom and lunchroom facilities than those that are less labor-intensive.

Location

Location may also be an important factor in determining the desirability of a particular property. Some industrial tenants require close proximity to their raw materials. Others require close proximity to their customers. Some prefer to be located in a heavily-populated area, to be assured of a good labor supply. If a plant uses hazardous, odorous, or noisy manufacturing processes, the preferred location would be away from heavily-populated areas. The nature of the business would also determine the need for access to highways, railways, marine terminals, or airports.

In many industries, there is a preference for locating close to industrial activity with similar characteristics. This tends to reduce the potential for appreciation in the land because it cannot be recycled to other uses.

Leases

Industrial leases are usually triple net with the lessee assuming responsibility for taxes, insurance, and maintenance. It would be unusual for an industrial lease to be indexed for inflation. Specific nonremovable improvements desired by the lessee are usually made at the lessee's expense with the premises to be returned in the same condition received.

The most important characteristic of tenants is their credit. The rate of insolvency among manufacturers is astoundingly high. Small manufacturers are particularly susceptible to this problem. Changes in overall economic conditions, changes in consumer taste, the entry of new competitors into the industry, and increasing raw material prices can turn a healthy income statement to red ink overnight. Most manufacturing firms cannot sustain operational losses for an extended period of time, and they either go bankrupt or retrench. Because industrial property is so use-specific, tenants that wish to renegotiate leases because the business is failing are in a strong position. A bankrupt tenant not only means lost revenue, but the property can be tied up by bankruptcy proceedings for a considerable period of time.

General Investment Characteristics

Strengths

Low Risk. The risk of investing in industrial real estate is directly related to the strength of the tenants and the demand for the specific property. The financial strength of a tenant depends on its ability to collateralize the lease or on the underlying viability of that firm and its industry. The demand for the specific property depends on local industrial conditions.

Cash Flow. The depreciable component of industrial property is often large relative to land costs. Where demand conditions permit the investor to maintain high occupancy rates, the project will yield a strong cash flow relative to its income.

Ease of Management. As long as tenants are stable, industrial properties tend to manage themselves. Upkeep and maintenance expenses are minimal. Industrial firms typically provide whatever services they require themselves.

Property Value Independent of Neighborhood. The functional nature of industrial property, and its tendency to be dedicated to a particular purpose once put to this function, tends to insulate the value of the property from shifting land-use patterns in its locale.

Weaknesses

Lack of Liquidity. Industrial property tends to be very use-specific. Converting industrial property to commercial or residential use is frequently difficult because of location, zoning laws, or building characteristics.

Obsolescence. Industrial patterns in the United States have changed significantly over the past two decades, and these changes may continue. The shoe manufacturing industry has passed and high-tech light manufacturing has arrived. In addition, the technology of production itself has undergone significant change likely to continue. A building constructed for an industry that no longer exists or a technology no longer used often loses a significant portion of its value.

Rent Risk. Each of the past three decades has seen a fall in manufacturing employment by at least 25 percent. The rapid pace of technological change, rapid changes in markets, and the specter of international competition has forced many industrial firms out of business. In manufacturing, a history of success is no guarantee of future success. When a tenant is no longer economically viable, the landlord often suffers financially as well.

Exposure to Environmental Regulations. In a society increasingly conscious of its environment, what is an acceptable standard of waste treatment today may be ruled unacceptable *ex post facto*. The owner of an industrial property may find its value diminished because of changing environmental regulations. Finding oneself owning contaminated land or land that contains some environmental threat because of past land use practices can expose an investor to considerable liability.

Tax Considerations

In many localities it is possible to secure financing on favorable terms through industrial revenue bonds. Industrial revenue bonds are issued by local or state governments to secure financing for industrial purposes on favorable terms. The favorable terms take the form of a lower interest rate available because the government agency puts its credit behind the bond and the interest from the bond receives favorable tax treatment. This particular advantage has been weakened by the Tax Reform Act of 1986 (TRA) because of the alternative minimum tax, but this form of financing continues to be an advantage.

Local governments issue industrial revenue bonds because of the substantial benefits accruing to the locality as a result of increased industrial activity. This attribute of industrial property may be used to reduce or eliminate property taxes in negotiating with local authorities. Industrial buildings and improvements may be depreciated over 31.5 years.

Case Study

Acquisition Phase. The hypothetical industrial real estate investment is a small industrial park in a rural area, located at the intersection of a railway line and a new interstate highway. The impetus for the project is from an investor who is able to obtain a lease on a build-to-suit from an absolute blue-chip company at the proposed location.

The anchor lease is for a 40,000-square-foot building that can be constructed at $60 per square foot. The tenant is willing to sign a 30-year lease that will fully amortize the building for $1.45 per square foot per month. The lease will be triple net with the tenant bearing the responsibility for taxes, insurance, and maintenance.

The land is purchased for $350,000. Expecting the demand for industrial facilities at this location to grow, the investor constructs a second 20,000-square-foot building (at a cost of $50 per square foot) that may be used for a variety of light manufacturing facilities. In addition, the investor constructs two 30,000-square-foot warehouses at a cost of $40 per square foot. The investor spends an additional $250,000 on improvements to the property—roads, lighting, and landscaping. The project is financed by the local county issuing industrial revenue bonds for $5,000,000. The bonds are to be amortized over 25 years at 8 percent. The investor provides the remaining capital necessary. Table 16.1 presents the sources and uses of funds.

Table 16.1 Sources and Uses of Funds

Sources of funds	
Equity	$1,500,000
Industrial bonds	5,000,000
Total sources	$6,500,000
Uses of funds	
Land costs	$ 350,000
Utilities/roads	250,000
Legal fees	100,000
Building #1	2,400,000
Building #2	1,000,000
Warehouses	2,400,000
Total uses	$6,500,000

Holding Phase. The first year of the project, only the 40,000-square-foot building is leased.

The second year a tenant is secured for the 20,000-square-foot building. The lease is triple net for 15 years at $1.25 per square foot per month with an annual percentage increase of 4 percent. In addition, 10,000 square feet of warehouse space is leased at a rate of $0.75 per square foot per month. The lease is double net with respect to maintenance and insurance.

In the third and subsequent years, the original tenants in the industrial buildings are retained. An average of 50,000 square feet of warehouse space is leased annually. The average rate in the third year is $0.85 per square foot per month and this rate increments 3 percent annually. All warehouse leases are double net.

Common ground maintenance expenses (landscaping, snowplowing, etc.) and property taxes are 12 percent of gross revenues. Table 16.2 shows the impact of this activity on income.

The income statement also reveals how tax savings work under the TRA. The loss of $96,375 in year one generates a potential reduction in tax liability of $26,985. If the investor is in the 28-percent bracket and has no other passive income, his or her adjusted gross income may only be reduced by $25,000, yielding a $7,500 tax saving. This means that the investor carries forward $19,485 in tax savings. In year two, taxable income from the project is positive and substantial. This would be considered passive income, so the entire tax savings may be realized as the unused $71,375 loss ($91,375 minus $25,000) may be used to lower passive income without limit.

In contrast to income, cash flows indicated in Table 16.3 on page 200 are positive throughout the holding period. Cash flows are also significantly larger than income throughout the period owing to the impact of substantial depreciation expense.

Disposal Phase. The industrial park is sold to an MLP at the end of ten years for $8,464,167 (or about 10 times pre-tax income). Associated selling costs to the investor are 3 percent of the sales price. This transaction yields an after-tax cash flow of $3,145,609.

The tax liability and after-tax cash flows are developed in Tables 16.4 (on page 200) and 16.5 (on page 201) respectively.

Table 16.2 Income Statement—Industrial Park

Year	1	2	3	4	5
Revenues:					
Building #1	$552,000	$552,000	$552,000	$552,000	$552,000
Building #2	0	300,000	309,000	318,270	327,818
Warehouses	0	90,000	510,000	525,300	541,059
Total revenues:	$552,000	$942,000	$1,371,000	$1,395,570	$1,420,877
Operating ex:					
Operating costs	$66,240	$113,040	$164,520	$167,468	$170,505
Interest expense	397,635	392,202	386,318	379,946	373,045
Depreciation	184,500	196,800	196,800	196,800	196,800
Total expenses	$648,375	$702,042	$747,638	$744,214	$740,350
Taxable income	($96,375)	$239,958	$623,362	$651,356	$680,527
Tax liability	($26,985)	$67,188	$174,541	$182,380	$190,548
Carry forward	($19,485)	$0	$0	$0	$0

Year	6	7	8	9	10
Revenues:					
Building #1	$552,000	$552,000	$552,000	$552,000	$552,000
Building #2	337,653	347,782	358,216	368,962	380,031
Warehouses	557,291	574,009	591,230	608,967	627,236
Total revenues:	$1,446,943	$1,473,792	$1,501,445	$1,529,929	$1,559,267
Operating ex:					
Operating costs	$173,633	$176,855	$180,173	$183,591	$187,112
Interest expense	365,572	357,478	348,712	339,219	328,938
Depreciation	196,800	196,800	196,800	196,800	196,800
Total expenses	$736,005	$731,133	$725,685	$719,610	$712,850
Taxable income	$710,938	$742,659	$775,760	$810,318	$846,417
Tax liability	$199,063	$207,944	$217,213	$226,889	$236,997

Table 16.3 Cash Flow Statement—Industrial Park

Year	1	2	3	4	5
Revenues:					
Building #1	$552,000	$552,000	$552,000	$552,000	$552,000
Building #2	0	300,000	309,000	318,270	327,818
Warehouses	0	90,000	510,000	525,300	541,059
Total revenues:	$552,000	$942,000	$1,371,000	$1,395,570	$1,420,877
Cash ex:					
Operating costs	66,240	113,040	164,520	167,468	170,505
Debt repayment	463,090	463,090	463,090	463,090	463,090
Total expenses	$529,330	$576,130	$627,610	$630,558	$633,595
Cash flow	$22,670	$365,870	$743,390	$765,012	$787,282

Year	6	7	8	9	10
Revenues:					
Building #1	$552,000	$552,000	$552,000	$552,000	$552,000
Building #2	337,653	347,782	358,216	368,962	380,031
Warehouses	557,291	574,009	591,230	608,967	627,236
Total revenues:	$1,446,943	$1,473,792	$1,501,445	$1,529,929	$1,559,267
Cash ex:					
Operating costs	173,633	176,855	180,173	183,591	187,112
Debt repayment	463,090	463,090	463,090	463,090	463,090
Total expenses	$636,723	$639,945	$643,263	$646,681	$650,202
Cash flow	$810,220	$833,847	$858,182	$883,247	$909,065

Table 16.4 Tax Calculation—Industrial Park

Net sale price	$8,210,242
Less:	
Adjusted basis	4,544,300
Taxable income	3,665,942
Tax liability	1,026,464

Table 16.5 After Tax Net Cash Flow—Industrial Park

Sale Price	$8,464,167
Less:	
Closing costs	253,925
Mortgage balance	4,038,169
Tax liability	1,026,464
Net cash flow	$3,145,609

As can be shown in Table 16.6, the investment in the industrial park was robust, yielding an NPV at 21 percent of $749,707 and an IRR of almost 30 percent. The profitability of this project largely reflects the high occupancy rate of the industrial park within the holding period.

Table 16.6 Evaluation of Return—Industrial Park

Year	Reversion	Tax Effect	Cash Flow	Cumulative Flows
0				($1,500,000)
1		$7,500	$22,670	30,170
2		(47,703)	365,870	318,167
3		(174,541)	743,390	568,849
4		(182,380)	765,012	582,632
5		(190,548)	787,282	596,734
6		(199,063)	810,220	611,158
7		(207,944)	833,847	625,902
8		(217,213)	858,182	640,969
9		(226,889)	883,247	656,358
10	$3,145,609	(236,997)	909,065	3,817,677
	$0	($1,675,777)	$6,978,784	$6,948,616

NPV_{21} = $749,787
IRR = 29.7%

Summary

Investment in industrial properties is potentially rewarding to aggressive investors. The lure of high returns is offset by the presence of high risk. A thorough analysis of patterns of industrial growth is critical to evaluating the potential for success in a particular industrial property.

For aggressive investors, the possibility of above-average returns is more than balanced by the lack of liquidity, danger of obsolescence, exposure to environmental regulation, and the potential variability in rents. While industrial property investment is clearly not for the novice, many small investors with good business sense will find opportunities in industrial properties worth pursuing.

Chapter 17

Mobile Home Parks

Mobile home parks offer investors excellent opportunities for cash flow and appreciation. There appears to be a long-term trend toward increasing demand for mobile homes, and many communities are reluctant to permit the new construction or expansion of existing mobile home parks. This situation suggests that rental fees for mobile home sites will rise subtantially in the future.

There are three basic types of mobile home parks: small old-fashioned parks; larger, modern mobile home parks; and resort mobile home parks. Mobile home parks consist primarily of land which may be improved by the presence of utility hookups, concrete pads, and rudimentary roads. However, mobile home parks many include many more amenities—expensive landscaping, common recreation areas, swimming pools, tennis courts, clubhouse, and shops.

The old-fashioned parks with 10 to 30 units and few amenities tend to be somewhat run down. These make excellent investments because of their relatively low acquisition cost and the potential for upgrading the rent structure. While a deteriorated mobile home park is not attractive, the costs of improvements such as cleaning up, landscaping, converting single slabs to double-wide slabs, and adding amenities are generally low, relative to the potential for rent increases. Parks in this category may frequently be purchased for gross rent multiples of five or six.

Modern parks of fifty to several hundred units boasting substantial amenities would normally be available for gross rent multiples in the 8 to 12 range, depending on location and local market conditions. These may still be good investments, however, because the demand for this type of residential unit may keep upward pressure on rents within the foreseeable future.

Mobile home parks in resort areas may also function as very handsome investments. Upward pressure on rents should arise from vacationers and retirees. The desirability of this type of park is very sensitive to the general viability of the resort in which it is located.

Demand for Mobile Homes

Mobile homes offer several advantages over conventional housing for many individuals. The advantages lie in lower acquisition costs, lower maintenance costs, and ease of upkeep. Modern mobile homes are not particularly mobile, requiring significant time and expense to move. A modern double-wide with two bathrooms, three bedrooms, and more than 1,400 square feet of living space can be purchased for under $30,000. Financing is readily available with 20-percent down for 15 years. Unit construction, modern materials, and aluminum or vinyl siding drastically reduce maintenance costs compared to conventional housing. In many localities, mobile homes are not subject to property taxes. The compact, single-floor layout of a mobile home is often particularly appealing to elderly people.

The cost advantages associated with this type of personal residence appeals to young single people, young married couples, divorced individuals, retirees, transient individuals (military or construction personnel), students, seasonal workers in resort areas, and individuals with relatively low incomes in high-cost of living areas. Between the aging of the population, a continued high divorce rate, and the continued increase in the cost of conventional housing, the demand for space in mobile home communities can only increase.

Supply of Mobile Home Space

The opportunity to set up a mobile home on a residential lot or rural acreage is being increasingly restricted by zoning and planning boards for aesthetic reasons. Applications to such boards for new mobile home parks are frequently looked on with disfavor. This attitude often reflects an inaccurate sterotype of mobile homes and mobile home residents. In areas where mobile homes are not subject to property taxes, current tax-paying residents are prone to feel that such residents are not paying their fair share for community services.

The degree of resistance to mobile home park development in a given area can be determined by examining the number of permits issued in recent years relative to the size of the waiting lists to get into existing mobile home parks.

Whatever the degree of resistance, it is likely to exist in some form. Under these circumstances, the investor may reasonably expect demand to outpace supply.

Valuing a Mobile Home Park

The value of an investment in a mobile home park is measured by the income produced and the potential for appreciation.

The largest expense in developing a mobile home park is the land. For this reason, mobile home parks are frequently located on the fringe of urban areas or in out-of-the-way locations where the price of land is lower. This situation raises the possibility that as the community grows, the potential use of the land might change and the value of the land increase as a result.

The desirable attributes of a mobile home park for residential purposes are the same as those for conventional single-family housing or apartments. Access to transportation, neighborhood, public amenities, and closeness to employers and shopping are all considered in choosing a location.

A first indication of value to the investor would be the gross rent multiple. This should be analyzed to determine the potential for increasing rents should the property be purchased. High vacancy rates in established mobile home parks are unusual.

High vacancy rates in all mobile home parks in an area suggests a temporary oversupply or attitudes that this type of residence is not considered desirable in the community. Under the first circumstance, this might prove an excellent time to buy. Current oversupply conditions may discourage existing owners about the prospects for the success of their investment and create great opportunities for investors who have confidence that the demand for this type of residence will increase over time.

In most communities, there is a shortage of mobile home space. This situation makes it easy to adjust rents up to reflect true market conditions. Money spent on upgrades frequently returns large dividends in rent increases.

General Investment Characteristics

Strengths

Potential for High Gain. Income and cash flows tend to increase over time as demand rises relative to supply. Operating costs are minimal. Where the land is located in the path of urban growth, the value of the land itself may increase substantially.

Ease of Acquisition. Capital requirements are generally lower than for other types of multiple-family residences. Financing for a mobile home park with a good rental history is generally available on favorable terms.

Lack of Management Responsibilities. The parks are generally of sufficient size to permit the use of professional management. Operating responsibilities are small, simplifing the management task (no air conditioners to break down or leaking pipes to fix).

Weaknesses

Finding an Appropriate Project. The potentials are so good in this area that future returns are already capitalized in the price of mobile home parks. Finding a good value may require an exhaustive search.

Community Resistance. Community resistance to mobile home parks may increase legal fees, make getting variances or zoning changes difficult, and result in an inadequate level of public services. Community resistance may be based on an outdated understanding of mobile home parks and can be countered by education.

Tax Considerations
As the value of land generally exceeds the value of improvements in mobile home parks, depreciation will not be large relative to the size of the investment, limiting the tax advantages to be gained from this type of investment.

Case Study

Acquisition Phase. An investor searches diligently for an opportunity to invest in a mobile home park and discovers that all mobile home parks in the community have excessively long waiting lists. Prices for available mobile home parks reflect this, running gross rent multiples of 15 to 20. The investor rejects these as unrealistic prices.

The investor explores the possibility of developing a mobile park independently but finds that the local zoning body will not permit any developments of this type in the near future.

The investor then discovers a mobile home park on the furthest fringes of the community that has 25 units, is badly run down, and is selling for more than 15 times gross rents. In the course of discussing the price of the park with the owner, the investor discovers the park is actually zoned for 50 units. The investor purchases the property for $270,000 ($150,000 cost of land) and expands $210,000 on improvements. The total investment of $480,000 is financed with a mortgage of $380,000, the mortgage to be amortized over 15 years at 10 percent.

The 25 units are fully rented for an average of $60 per unit per month. The investor spends $10,000 to repair a fence around the property, add a picnic area, and landscape the park. After six month, the investor raises rents for the units to $80. Five of the existing tenants leave immediately.

The cost of extending utilities, roads, and pouring double-wide concrete slabs for each of the 25 new units is $175,000. A new pool is added for $25,000. A local bank advances $160,000 toward these costs at a rate of 12 percent for 10 years. (Table 17.1 shows the sources and uses of funds.)

Table 17.1 Sources and Uses of Funds

Sources of funds	
Debt	$380,000
Equity	100,000
Total sources	$480,000
Uses of funds	
Purchase price	270,000
Improvements	210,000
Total uses	$480,000

Holding Phase. At the end of the first year, the rent for the 20 singles is raised to $110 per month and for the 30 double-wides to $150 per month. It is anticipated that after the first year, rents will increase 10 percent per year.

Operating expenses, including taxes and insurance, average 10 percent of revenues. Tables 17.2 and 17.3 present the income and cash flow statements for the project.

Table 17.2 Mobile Home Park Income Statement

Year	1	2	3	4	5
Rental income	$18,600	$80,400	$88,440	$97,284	$107,012
Operating ex:					
Direct costs	1,860	8,040	8,844	9,728	10,701
Depr	11,550	10,560	10,560	10,560	10,560
Interest	45,081	43,857	42,479	40,925	39,175
Profit (loss)	($39,891)	$17,943	$26,557	$36,071	$46,576
Taxes	($11,169)	$5,024	$7,436	$10,100	$46,576

Year	6	7	8	9	10
Rental income	$117,714	$129,485	$142,434	$156,677	$172,345
Operating ex:					
Direct costs	11,771	12,949	14,243	15,668	17,234
Depr	10,560	10,560	10,560	10,560	10,560
Interest	37,202	34,780	32,475	29,653	26,473
Profit (loss)	$58,180	$71,197	$85,155	$100,796	$118,077
Taxes	$16,290	$19,935	$23,843	$28,223	$33,062

Table 17.3 Mobile Home Park Cash Flow Statement

Year	1	2	3	4	5
Rental income	$18,600	$80,400	$88,440	$97,284	$107,012
Operating ex:					
Direct costs	1,860	8,040	8,844	9,728	10,701
Debt service	54,728	54,728	54,728	54,728	54,728
Cash flow	($37,988)	$17,632	$24,868	$32,828	$41,583

Year	6	7	8	9	10
Rental income	$117,714	$129,485	$142,434	$156,677	$172,345
Operating ex:					
Direct costs	11,771	12,949	14,243	15,668	17,234
Debt service	54,728	54,728	54,728	54,728	54,728
Cash flow	$51,214	$61,809	$73,462	$86,281	$100,382

The project shows a substantial loss the first year as a result of the high price paid for the park and the loss of some revenue through renter turnover. Income quickly turns positive as the newly created units are rented, reflecting the ability of dollars expanded on this type of investment to generate substantial returns. Cash flows show a similar pattern.

Disposal Phase. At the end of ten years the property is sold for $1,800,000 to a developer who will use it for a shopping center. Tables 17.4, 17.5, and 17.6 present the tax liability and resultant basis calculations. The net cash flow from this transaction is $1,117,772.

Table 17.4 Basis Calculation

Cost of property	$480,000
Less depreciation	106,590
Adjusted basis	$373,410

Table 17.5 Tax Schedule

Net sales	$1,692,000
Adjusted basis	373,410
Gain on sale	$1,318,590
Tax liability	369,205
After-tax return	$ 949,385

Table 17.6 Net After-Tax Cash Flow

Selling price	$1,800,000
Less:	
Selling commission	108,000
Mortgage commission	205,023
Taxes	369,205
Net cash flow	$1,117,772

The investor earns an IRR of 33 percent from the initial $100,000 invest-
ment. At a 21-percent rate of discount, the total return depicted in Table 17.7
is found to have a NPV of $481,361.

Table 17.7 Evaluation of Return

Year	Cash Flow	After-Tax Reversion	Taxes	Total
0				$(100,000)
1	$(37,98)		$(11,169)	(26,819)
2	17,632		5,024	12,608
3	24,868		7,436	17,432
4	32,828		10,100	22,728
5	41,583		13,041	28,542
6	51,214		16,290	34,924
7	61,809		19,935	41,873
8	73,462		23,843	49,619
9	86,281		28,223	58,058
10	100,382	$1,117,772	33,062	1,185,092
	$452,071		$145,785	$1,324,058

IRR = 32.8%
NPV_{12} = $481,361

Summary

Mobile home parks present unusually good investment opportunities as a
result of community-imposed constraints on their construction and underlying increases in demand. Over the past decade, appreciation in the value of
this type of real estate has exceeded most other real estate investment forms.
At the present time, most mobile home park owners are fully aware of the
value of their property and, when available, mobile home parks are fully
priced.

In the absence of rent controls, an investor in mobile home parks may
reasonably expect the market to sustain strong increases in rent levels. This
will increase cash flows and provide the investor with appreciation in the
value of the property as well.

Chapter 18

Low-Income Housing

The impact of the Tax Reform Act of 1986 on real estate investing is generally considered negative by investors. The reduction in the individual's top marginal tax rate to 28 percent coupled with an increase in the write-off period for depreciation to 27.5 years for residential properties has lessened the attractiveness of many real estate investments.

The Tax Credit for Low Income Rental Housing Program in the Tax Reform Act provides an important exception to this generalization. This program offers the sophisticated investor an opportunity for tax shelter and significant returns. The Program began in 1987 and, under current law, extends only through 1989. While the thrust and effect of the Tax Reform Act was to provide a simpler and more equitable tax system by eliminating tax "loopholes," this innovative program moves in a different direction in order to accomplish the social goal of stimulating the supply of low-income housing. The law itself is exceptionally complex and couples the potential for higher gains with higher risks.

The program is designed to aid new construction, the acquisition of existing properties, and the rehabilitation of existing properties. Qualifying housing can range from a single room or a single-family rental property to a multi-building apartment complex. Units in a project qualify for the tax credit under this program by having the tenants of the unit meet an income test. Units may not be substandard and must comply with all building codes. Tenants cannot be transient (defined as not having an initial lease for six months or longer). Property with one unit occupied by an owner (or relation), a building with four units, sanitariums, lifecare facilities, retirement homes and trailer parks are also excluded from coverage under this program.

The effective use of this program will be significantly increased by coupling its implementation with other facets of federal and state housing programs. Grants for the purchase of land and/or buildings, access to capital, capital below market rates, rent supplements, and property tax concessions may be available to the investor in low-income properties who aggressively seeks aid.

As with any real estate investment, the ultimate value of a low-income property is largely determined by its underlying economic viability. The investor needs to carefully consider the timing of the costs and benefits associated with the project through the acquisition, holding, and disposal stages of ownership. The desirability of investing in a low-income property is influenced by an array of market forces: current and future supply of low-income housing, current and future demand for low-income housing, cost of capital, cost and difficulty of rehabilitating and/or maintaining low-income property, expense and effort associated with managing this type of property, and potential for appreciation in the underlying land.

Benefits

The specific incentive provided by this program is a tax credit based on the cost of qualifying rental units as shown in Table 18.1.

Table 18.1 Available Tax Credits Under the Tax Credit for Low-Income Housing Program

Activity	10-year Credit (%)[1]
Building Acquisition	4
New Construction	9
Major Rehabilitation (> $2000)	9
Minor Rehabilitation (< $2000)	4
Federally subsidized new construction or rehabilitation[2]	4

[1]The applicable credit in 1987. This percentage is applied to the qualifying basis annually for ten successive years, effectively returning to investors a present value equal to 70 percent (where the credit is 9 percent) or 30 percent (where the credit is 4 percent) of their qualifying basis. The applicable credit in 1988 and 1989 will be determined in such a manner as to return the same present value to the investor.

[2]Where the cost of capital is subsidized by another federal housing program. Investors may elect to exclude the amount of subsidy from the qualifying basis and thus regain the 9-percent credit rate if otherwise appropriate.

These tax credits are fully applicable on a dollar-for-dollar basis against other passive income. The tax credits may also be applied dollar-for-dollar against tax liability arising from ordinary income up to $7,500 for a joint return in the 28-percent tax bracket, or up to $8,333 for a joint return in the

33-percent tax bracket. This amount is reduced $1 for every $6 by which the investor's adjusted gross income exceeds $200,000. This tax credit can be used to offset tax liability from ordinary income only if adjusted gross income is under $250,000. If an investor has unused tax credits, they can be carried forward for use in the future or until the property is sold. Any unused tax credits at that time can be used to offset any gain from the sale of the property. As with any property, losses carried forward by the investor can be applied against both ordinary and passive income at the time of sale.

Restrictions

State Limitations. Through its designated housing agency, each state can issue tax credits up to a total of $1.25 per resident per year. This represents a potential of $300,000,000 annual tax credit. As a result of the innovative nature of this program, investors have been slow to develop projects, and this limitation has not been a problem.

Time. Although the tax credit itself only extends for ten years, projects must retain the low-income units which comprised the qualifying basis for tax credit over a 15-year period, or they are subject to proportionate recapture of tax credits.

Proportion. Any proportion of a project may be used as qualified low-income housing if the tenants meet an income test. If the project is less than 100-percent low-income housing, a proportional tax credit is granted according to the number of low-income units relative to the total number of units in the project or the number of square feet used for low-income housing relative to the total number of square feet in the project.

Present Income Test. Tenants in qualified housing must meet certain income limitation tests. To qualify a project, 20 percent of the residents must have incomes lower than 50 percent of the regional median income or 40 percent of the residents must have incomes lower than 60 percent of the regional median income. The appropriate level of income is adjusted for family size. The Department of Housing and Urban Development (HUD) publishes regional income data annually.

Future Income Test. Continuous compliance with the income limitations for qualifying units over a 15-year period is necessary to avoid penalties and the recapture of prior tax credit. Protection against loss of compliance through rising tenant income is contained in a provision allowing tenant incomes to rise 40 percent above the minimum level, provided that tenants initially met the income test. Further, if a tenant's income increases above this level, the project will remain in compliance as long as the next comparable vacant unit is rented to a tenant who meets the income test. This means that a 100-percent qualified low-income project should always be in compliance as the next available unit will be rented out to a low-income tenant.

Rent Limitation. Rents cannot be higher than 30 percent of the maximum income allowed for a given tenant. The definition of rent includes utilities. If the utilities are paid by the tenant, the maximum rent allowed is adjusted by a published utility factor for the region. For most communities, this effectively means that rent (with tenant-paid utilities) cannot be higher than 25 percent of the minimum qualifying income level. HUD Section 8 rent subsidies are *not* included in this limitation.

This limitation does not appear overly restrictive. Table 18.2 indicates national median income levels for 1986.

Table 18.2 Four-Person Household Median Income and Gross Rent Levels—1986

	Maximum Income Level	Maximum Gross Rent
50% Level	$13,750	$334
60% Level	16,500	412

General Investment Characteristics

Strengths

Recovery of Costs. The investor is effectively able to recover as much as 70 percent of the costs of low-income rental units over a ten-year period. If the project is leveraged, the investor can quickly recover the initial capital expenses.

Potential Profits. Even under conditions of high tenant turnover, high maintenance expenses, and rent caps tied to regional income levels, the recovery of such a substantial portion of initial costs can make this type of project an attractive investment. Profitably may be further enhanced through the use of Section 8 rent subsidies, and a variety of federal, state, and private programs addressing the needs of the disadvantaged in our society.

Potential Appreciation. Depending on the location of the property and the pattern of urban growth, the property can appreciate significantly in value over the 15-year period. This is particularly true if the property is upgraded to provide housing for more affluent tenants or converted to commercial or industrial use.

Weaknesses

Loss of Liquidity. Once an investor takes a tax credit for a low-income housing project, he or she is committed to maintaining the low-income units in the project as low-income units for at least 15 years. If the project is sold sooner than that, the seller must post a bond to ensure continued compliance.

Management Problems. Residential rental investment properties frequently require some management involvement on the part of the investor. This is more of a problem with low-income rental housing, partly because professional property management companies generally do not like to work with this type of property. Direct personal involvement may require more time and effort from the investor than anticipated. One way to overcome this difficulty would be to find a public or private service agency experienced with addressing the needs of poor people to manage the property.

Project Documentation. The complex and innovative nature of the Low-Income Housing Tax Credit Program raise numerous questions about how the program should be implemented and operated: Exactly how shall tenant incomes be verified? What happens to income levels when family structure changes? It is hard to determine the cost of documenting and certifying that the tax law requirements are met.

Tax Considerations

The wide range of properties covered by this portion of the TRA allows investors to tailor the size of the project to their particular tax situations. Under current tax provisions, investors in the 28-percent bracket would be able to realize a maximum of $83,333 tax credit over the 10-year period to be applied against ordinary income. The amount of tax credit that could be applied against the tax liability on passive income is unlimited. Unused tax credits may be carried forward.

Case Study

Acquisition Phase. Suppose an investor has ordinary income of $120,000 per year and purchases for $42,500 a severely deteriorated five-unit apartment in a low-income neighborhood adjacent to the central business district. Then the investor rehabilitates the property to meet all code requirements for $55,000, which yields a final cost per unit (CPU) of $20,000.

Table 18.3 Sources and Uses of Funds

Capital required	
Cost of property (land at $7,500)	$ 42,500
Rehabilitation costs	55,000
Additional closing costs	2,500
Total capital required:	$100,000
Sources of capital	
Mortgage (10% for 30 years)	$ 75,000
Investor's capital	25,000
Total capital provided:	$100,000

The 80-percent anticipated occupancy rate includes the time necessary for rehabilitation. Relatively high tenant turnover and associated maintenance costs are anticipated. The use of Section 8 rent subsidies are not included, although this would certainly improve the project's income and cash flow characteristics.

Holding phase. To finance the purchase and rehabilitation, the investor put up $25,000 in equity and secured the balance with a mortgage for

$75,000 amortized over a period of 30 years at 10 percent per annum (see Table 18.4). The annual debt servicing requirement will be $7,898.16, and the investor plans to hold the property for 15 years. The selling price is expected to be $134,000.

Table 18.4 Loan Amortization Schedule $75,000 30-Year Loan (10%)

Year	Total Interest	Principal Payment	Total Payment	Remaining Balance
1	$7,481.23	$ 416.93	$7,898.16	$74,583.07
2	7,437.56	460.60	7,898.16	74,122.47
3	7,389.36	508.80	7,898.16	73,613.66
4	7,336.07	562.09	7,898.16	73,051.58
5	7,277.22	620.94	7,898.16	72,430.65
6	7,212.20	685.96	7,898.16	71,744.68
7	7,140.36	757.80	7,898.16	70,986.88
8	7,061.00	837.16	7,898.16	70,149.71
9	6,973.35	924.81	7,898.16	69,224.90
10	6,876.49	1,021.67	7,898.16	68,203.23
11	6,769.51	1,128.65	7,898.16	67,074.58
12	6,651.33	1,246.83	7,898.16	65,827.76
13	6,520.77	1,377.39	7,898.16	64,450.36
14	6,376.55	1,521.61	7,898.16	62,928.75
15	6,217.22	1,680.94	7,898.16	61,247.81
16	6,041.20	1,856.96	7,898.16	59,390.85
17	5,846.75	2,051.41	7,898.16	57,339.43
18	5,631.94	2,266.22	7,898.16	55,073.21
19	5,394.63	2,503.53	7,898.16	52,569.68
20	5,132.49	2,765.67	7,898.16	49,804.00
21	4,842.87	3,055.29	7,898.16	46,748.71
22	4,522.95	3,375.21	7,898.16	43,373.49
23	4,169.53	3,728.63	7,898.16	39,644.86
24	3,779.09	4,119.07	7,898.16	35,525.79
25	3,347.78	4,550.38	7,898.16	30,975.40
26	2,871.27	5,026.89	7,898.16	25,948.51
27	2,344.90	5,553.26	7,898.16	20,395.25
28	1,763.41	6.134.75	7,898.16	14,260.50
29	1,121.01	6,777.15	7,898.16	7,483.55
30	411.36	7,483,35	7,894.71	0

Rental income for the first year of the project is $11,040, reflecting an average rent of $230 per month per unit, and increases at a rate of 3 percent per year. Leasing expenses are 5 percent of rental income. Maintenance expenses and property taxes are $1,000 and $800 respectively in year one and increase at a rate of 4 percent per year. Insurance costs $325 the first year and increases at a rate of 6 percent per year.

Table 18.4 shows annual interest expense. The depreciation expense in year one is calculated by multiplying the appropriate depreciation percentage (i.e., 3.5 percent in the first year) by the sum of the cost of the existing structure ($37,500) plus the rehabilitation expenditures ($55,000). Thus, depreciation expense in year one is $3,238 (i.e., 3.5 percent times $92,500) over this period.

Taxable income or loss represents rental income less the sum of leasing expense, maintenance expense, property taxes, depreciation, and interest expense. The tax credit is equal to 4 percent of the purchase price and closing costs (excluding land costs) plus 9 percent of the renovation cost. The tax benefit (liability) equals the investor's taxable loss (income) times 33 percent plus the dollar amount of RTC (see Table 18.5).

Table 18.6 on page 224 shows the annual cash flow statement for the investment over the 15-year investment horizon. Net cash flow is found by subtracting the sum of all operating expenses (leasing, maintenance, insurance expenses, and property taxes) and debt servicing requirements from rental income. Cash flow is positive during the first eight years of the project, while income is negative. This occurs because of the combined effect of tax savings resulting from the tax credit and depreciation expense.

Disposal phase. The property appreciates at an annual rate of 3 percent over the 15-year period and sells for $134,400 plus closing costs of 5 percent. The basis of the property, as calculated in Table 18.7 on page 225, is the initial purchase price plus nonexpensed closing costs less the sum of annual depreciation expense over the 15-year period.

The taxable income—$77,538—is determined by subtracting the adjusted basis from the net sale price ($127,680—the gross sale price less closing costs). If the applicable tax rate is 33 percent, the tax liability is $25,587.

Having established the adjusted basis and the tax liability, we can calculate after-tax cash flow by subtracting the sum of closing costs ($6,720), remaining mortgage balance at the end of year 15 ($61,248), and taxes ($25,587) from the gross sale price of $134,400 (see Table 18.8, page 225).

Table 18.5   Income Statement—Low Income Housing Project

Year	1	2	3	4	5	6	7
Rental income	$11,040	$11,371	$11,712	$12,064	$12,426	$12,798	$13,182
Less:							
Leasing	552	569	586	603	621	640	659
Maintenance	1,000	1,040	1,082	1,125	1,170	1,217	1,265
Insurance	325	345	365	387	410	435	461
Property	800	832	865	900	936	973	1,012
Depr	3,238	3,330	3,330	3,330	3,330	3,330	3,330
Interest	7,481	7,438	7,389	7,336	7,277	7,212	7,140
Profit (loss)	($2,356)	($2,182)	($1,904)	($1,617)	($1,319)	($1,008)	($685)
Tax credit	6,450	6,450	6,450	6,450	6,450	6,450	6,450
Tax effect	$7,227	$7,170	$7,078	$6,984	$6,885	$6,783	$6,676

Year	8	9	10	11	12	13	14	15
Rental income	$13,578	$13,985	$14,405	$14,837	$15,282	$15,740	$16,213	$16,699
Less:								
Leasing	679	699	720	742	764	787	811	835
Maintenance	1,316	1,369	1,423	1,480	1,539	1,601	1,665	1,732
Insurance	489	518	549	582	617	654	693	735
Property	1,053	1,095	1,139	1,184	1,232	1,281	1,332	1,385
Depr	3,330	3,330	3,330	3,330	3,330	3,330	3,330	3,330
Interest	7,061	6,973	6,876	6,770	6,651	6,521	6,377	6,217
Profit (loss)	($349)	$1	$367	$749	$1,149	$1,567	$2,005	$2,465
Tax effect	$6,565	$6,450	$6,329	($247)	($379)	($517)	($662)	($814)

Table 18.6 Cash Flow Statement—Low Income Housing Project

Year	1	2	3	4	5	6	7
Rental income	$11,040	$11,371	$11,712	$12,064	$12,426	$12,798	$13,182
Leasing	552	569	586	603	621	640	659
Maint	1,000	1,040	1,082	1,125	1,170	1,217	1,265
Insurance	325	345	365	387	410	435	461
Property	800	832	865	900	936	973	1,012
Debt	7,898	7,898	7,898	7,898	7,898	7,898	7,898
Cash flow	$465	$688	$917	$1,151	$1,390	$1,636	$1,887

Year	8	9	10	11	12	13	14	15
Rental income	$13,578	$13,985	$14,405	$14,837	$15,282	$15,740	$16,213	$16,699
Leasing	679	699	720	742	764	787	811	835
Maint	1,316	1,369	1,423	1,480	1,539	1,601	1,665	1,732
Insurance	489	518	549	582	654	693	693	735
Property	1,053	1,095	1,139	1,184	1,232	1,281	1,332	1,385
Debt	7,898	7,898	7,898	7,898	7,898	7,898	7,898	7,898
Cash flow	$2,144	$2,406	$2,675	$2,951	$3,232	$3,520	$3,814	$4,114

Table 18.7 Basis Calculation

Acquisition costs	$ 97,500
Plus:	
Closing costs	2,500
	$100,000
Less:	
Accumulated depreciation	49,857
Adjusted basis	$ 50,143

Table 18.8 After-Tax Cash Flow

Selling price		$134,400
Less:		
Selling expenses(5%)	$ 6,720	
Mortgage balance	61,248	
Tax liability	25,857	
		$ 93,555
After-tax cash flow		$ 40,845

The after-tax rate of return is composed of three components: the project's cash flow during the investment phase; the tax effects over the holding phase; and the after-tax reversion. The after-tax rate of return (IRR) on the $25,000 of invested capital is 31.6 percent and yields a NPV discounted at 21 percent of $11,609 (see Table 18.9).

Summary

The Tax Credit for Low-Income Housing Program provides substantial incentives for investment in low-income housing. For an investor who has tax liability that can be offset by the tax credits generated, the return on a low-income project is potentially outstanding. To capture these gains, the investor must be willing to make a long-term commitment to the project and find a mechanism to adequately resolve the property management problem.

Table 18.9 Evaluation of Return

Year	Net Cash Effect	Tax Benefit	Cash Flow In	Reversion
0	$(25,000)			
1	7,692	$7,227	$ 465	
2	7,858	7,170	688	
3	7,995	7,078	917	
4	8,134	6,984	1,151	
5	8,275	6,885	1,390	
6	8,418	6,783	1,636	
7	8,563	6,676	1,887	
8	8,709	6,565	2,144	
9	8,856	6,450	2,406	
10	9,004	6,329	2,675	
11	2,704	(247)	2,951	
12	2,853	(379)	3,232	
13	3,003	(517)	3,520	
14	3,152	(662)	3,814	
15	44,145	(814)	4,114	$40,844.62
	$114,362	$65,529	$32,988	$40,844.62

IRR = 31.6%
NPV_{21} = $11,609

Chapter 19

The Financial Analysis of Real Estate Limited Partnerships: A Model Software System[*]

Real estate limited partnerships are complex financial vehicles which offer great opportunities to investors. Computer software systems similar to the one outlined in this article are a timesaving device that allows the analyst to explore in greater detail the underlying assumptions that are the basis for return measures. The need for a reliable system such as this is evidence by the volume of successful lawsuits brought by limited partners proving that these investments have not been screened properly by analysts in the past.

This system was developed by the author to facilitate analysis of real estate limited partnerships by providing a comprehensive system to properly evaluate these investment opportunities. This software system provides the analyst with a financial profile of real estate limited partnerships including multiple estimates of the partnership's return as well as the identification of those factors affecting return. The system is designed to be user friendly with its menu-driven feature while providing the user information essential for proper decision making.

The system provides the user a comprehensive profile of the limited partnership under review, including development of several real estate value and return measures as well as critical factors likely to affect the project's riskiness. In addition, the system allows the user to see how the partnership's return measures are affected by varying any of the underlying assumptions. This sensitivity analysis helps the analyst identify crucial variables that may determine the partnership's ultimate success.

System Overview

After entering the data requested in the input menu, the program will provide the user with several output statements. These reports include income statement, cash flow statement, and break- even analysis (profit/cash basis) as well as detailed profiles of the limited partnership's return/risk measures. All these reports can be accessed through the results menu, which is reproduced in Table 19.1.[1]

Although all the financial tools available in this system can't be highlighted, some of these features are discussed below.

Components of Limited Partnerships

The components of the limited partnership under consideration include the sources and uses of funds, the partnership fee structure, and the partnership sharing arrangement.

Sources and Uses of Funds Statement

Table 19.2 presents the sources and uses of funds statement for a hypothetical limited partnership. The sources of funds detail the amounts con-

Table 19.1 Results Menu

	Page No.
Income statement	10
Cash Flow statement	11
Pro forma statements	
Breakeven analysis of profits	12
Cash breakeven	13
Relative contribution	14
Return measures	15
Degree of leverage	16
Sources and uses of funds	17
Performance measures	17
Optimal holding period analysis	18
Key ratios	18
Exit	19

Table 19.2 Sources and Uses of Funds Statement

Sources		
LP contribution	$1,000,000	20%
GP contribution	50,000	5
Debt	3,950,000	75
Total Sources	$5,000,000	100%
Uses		
Real Estate	$3,500,000	70%
Land	500,000	10
Working capital	350,000	7
Other	650,000	13
Total Uses	$5,000,000	100%

tributed by both the limited and general partners as well as the amount to be raised by debt, in both dollar and percentage forms. Not only is the amount of the general partners' equity investment disclosed but also the degree to which borrowed funds are to be used in the venture itself.

The uses section of the statement will identify how the funds that are raised are to be used. In Table 19.2, 80 percent of the funds raised will be used to acquire the land and its improvements. An additional 7 percent of the funds will be applied to working capital reserves, and the remaining 13 percent will be consumed by acquisition-related expenses. Thus, in this example, approximately 87 percent of the funds being raised will be allocated between real estate and working capital. The analyst must focus on the remaining 13 percent to determine how much of these acquisition-related expenses are necessary. Remember, the less directly invested, the lower the limited partners' profit potential.

Analysis of partnership's fee structure.

The expected return to the limited partners is not only influenced by the percentage of funds raised that are actually invested but also by the amount of money diverted to general partners as fees. Table 19.3 reports the fees paid by the limited partnership during the acquisition, holding period, and disposal phases of the investment.

Table 19.3   Fee Structure

Phase:	
Acquisition	13%
Holding	6
Disposal	4

Acquisition Phase Fees. Selling commissions, offering fees, and other acquisition-related fees are included in this category. These are stated in terms of the percentage of total funds raised, and amount to 13 percent in our current example.

Holding Phase Fees. Management and leasing expenses, as well as other fees, are included in this group. These fees are stated as a percentage of rental income and/or assets under management. In our hypothetical limited partnership, these fees amount to 6 percent of rental income.

Disposal Phase Fees. Such fees include any disposal expense resulting from the sale of the partnership's assets. This would represent a percentage of the asset's sale price, which is 4 percent in our current example.

Partnership's Sharing Arrangement

The proposed sharing arrangement between the limited and general partners should be evaluated in terms of its fairness to all parties. The allocation of profit (losses), operating cash distributions, and reversionary cash distributions will have a direct impact on the limited partners' actual return.

A relationship should exist between the contributions of the partners and their share of any benefits. If the limited partners are to contribute all the equity capital for the venture, the sharing arrangement must be structured to ensure that they will be first in line to receive benefits from the partnership. The sharing arrangement must also ensure that these benefits are sufficient to reward the limited partners for their investment in the partnership.

Profile of the Investor's Return

Once these components of the limited partnership are understood, the analyst can then focus on estimating the return and risk characteristics of the investment under review based on his assumptions. To accomplish this, several return calculations can be made to provide a profile of the limited partnership's attractiveness. Table 19.4 reports five commonly used measures of investor's return.

Return on Investment (ROI). The return on investment represents the after-tax rate of return assuming that all net cash flows are reinvested at the limited partner's required rate of return. This measure allows the analyst to input his expected rate of return for all funds received while the partnership is in operation.

Net Present Value. The net present value (NPV) approach provides the analyst with the present dollar value of the investment. Under this approach, the investor's required rate of return becomes the hurdle rate on which the limited partnership investment is judged. The NPV approach assumes that cash flows are reinvested at the limited partner's required rate of return.

Internal Rate of Return. The internal rate of return (IRR) is similar to return on investment except that under this approach all cash flows are assumed to be reinvested at a rate equivalent to the IRR rather than at the investor's required rate of return. In using this return measure, the analyst must decide whether the cash flows can be reinvested at this return. If this is not possible, the analyst should then rely on the ROI measure.

Table 19.4   Return Measures

Return on investment	19.55%
Net present value	$2,010
Internal rate of return	20.00%
Average annual cash yield	5.53%
After-tax average return	4.23%

Average Annual Cash Yield. The average annual cash yield (AACY) measure provides a cash-on-cash measure of return which is calculated by dividing the projected average annual cash distributions by the limited partner's initial capital contribution. The AACY can be compared with current yields on competing investments to weigh its attractiveness on a current-yield basis.

In our example, the AACY is 5.53 percent. This low AACY relative to the higher total return measures (e.g., the ROI of 19.55 percent) suggests that the major contribution to return is due to property appreciation and/or assumed tax benefits.

After-tax Average Return. The after-tax average return (AAR) restates the AACY on an after-tax basis. This measure is calculated by dividing the projected cash distributions (plus tax benefits or less tax liabilities) by the limited partner's initial capital contribution. This measure is designed to allow the analyst to compare the limited partnership's yield to other investments on an after-tax basis.

Relative Contributions Toward Return

Although individuals may base their investment decision on the real estate limited partnership's expected return, proper evaluation requires identifying and clearly understanding the factors which contribute to return. As the previous return measures imply, several factors determine the return measures. Typically, return is based on the investment's cash distributions and tax benefits (or liabilities) during the operating phase and reversionary cash flows when the real estate is sold. Table 19.5 presents a breakdown of the limited partnership's return into its three components.

Table 19.5   Breakdown of Return Measure Components

Relative Contribution	NPV Amount	Percentage
Cash Flow	$13,403	29.30
Tax Benefits	($4,599)	(10.05)
Reversion	$36,937	80.75
Totals	$45,741	100.00

Although a return of 20 percent (see Table 19.4) may at first glance seem attractive, the analyst must look beyond this number and identify the relative contributions of each of these three components of return. For example, if the return is primarily attributed to the projected reversionary profits rather than the project's operating cash flows, the desired return will only be achieved if the real estate is sold at the assumed price. Under these circumstances, the analyst must closely examine the forecast sale price to determine whether it is reasonable.

Real Estate Value Indicators

To facilitate evaluation of the projected property's acquisition and sales prices, comparing the initial year's real estate value indicators to those calculated in the last year under the assumed sales price is helpful. If the terminal year's value indicators improve dramatically when compared to those measures reported initially, the sales price would be suspect. Table 19.6 reports three typical value measures for both the initial and terminal years.

Real Multiplier. The rent multiplier relates market value as a multiple of real estate property's rental income. The measure is calculated for both the first (acquisition phase) and last (disposal phase) years. This feature is important since it allows for not only current market comparison but serves as a check of the terminal year's sale price relative to the terminal year's projected rents as well. An increase form five times to nine times would suggest that the projected sales price is optimistic, stating it kindly.

Although many individuals may base their investment decision on the real estate limited partnership's expected return, proper evaluation re-

Table 19.6   Real Estate Value Indicators

Real Estate Value Indicator	Year	
	First	Last
Rent multiplier	5.00	9.00
Cost comparison (per sq. ft.)	$77.38	$126.05
Capitalization rates	10.14%	7.94%

quires identifying and clearly understanding the factors that contribute to return.

Cost Comparison Index. Another useful measure, the cost comparison index relates the market price at time of acquisition (first year) and disposal (last year) on a cost-per-square-foot basis. This measure provides additional information relating to the attractiveness of the investment at the beginning and end of the venture.

Capitalization Rate. The capitalization rate is found by dividing operating income by the assumed market price. The resulting capitalization rate can be compared with those of similar type properties. In our current illustration, the analyst would be prompted to investigate the reasons for such a dramatic drop in the property's capitalization rate.

Optimal Holding Period

Computer-assisted analysis allows the user to identify the optimal holding period of a real estate limited partnership under several assumptions. Table 19.7 reports the optimal holding period in terms of IRR and NPV criteria. The optimal holding period is simply the time period which maximizes the limited partner's return performance.

The optimal holding period provides several benefits. First, it reports the year in which the selected return measure is the highest. This feature is useful since the analyst can compare the expected return using the planned holding period with that obtained if the asset is held until the optimum return measure. The additional return can then be evaluated in light of the liquidity desires of the investor.

Second, this measure may provide information as to whether the general partner is acting in the interest of the limited partners. The general partner's compensation arrangement may be such that his holding-period

Table 19.7   Optimal Holding Period

	Amount	*Year*
IRR Criteria	22.35%	2010
NPV Criteria	$3,080	1995

objectives do not coincide with those of the limited partner. For example, the fee structure might be such that the general partner is compensated on the basis of assets under management. Thus, as long as the partnership is operating, the general partner, would receive fees regardless of the limited partners' own return performance. Thus, the optimal holding period analysis alerts the analyst to potential conflicts between the partners.

Profile of Investor's Risk

The previous section describes various return measures. Although paying attention to the forecast return of a real estate limited partnership is vital, risk must also be evaluated. This section will illustrate how computer-assisted real estate analysis can help investors identify potential problem areas which may adversely affect the limited partnership's return.

The sensitivity of the real estate project to changes in rental income is evaluated using several performance risk measures. Table 19.8 reports key performance measures which can help identify sources of risk or return shortfalls.

Degree of Operating Leverage. The first measure, degree of operating leverage (DOL), provides the analyst with a test of the limited partnership's operating risk by comparing the investment's fixed and variable costs at a given level of rental income. The higher the DOL, the greater the impact that fluctuating rental income will have on operating profits.

Real estate limited partnerships, due to their inherent capital intensity (higher fixed to total cost ratio), have a high degree of operating lever-

Table 19.8 Performance Risk Measures

Performance Measure

Degree of	
Operating leverage	1.38
Financial leverage	4.65
Projected rental income to breakeven rental income	74%
Projected rental income to cash breakeven	107%
Fixed costs/total costs	75%

age. For those limited partnerships with a high DOL, a slight change in vacancy levels will produce proportionately higher changes in operating income.

Degree of Financial Leverage. The degree of financial leverage (DFL) enables the analyst to gauge the additional risk introduced by partnership's use of borrowed funds. DFL measures the changes in pretax profits which result form increases of decreases in the partnership's operating income due to debt financing. The higher this leverage indicator, the greater financial risk.

Breakeven Rental Income to Forecast Rental Income. This measure provides the analyst with the percentage decrease in rental income before the project reports a loss from operations.

Cash Breakeven Rental Income to Forecast Rental Income. This measure provides information as to how far the actual rental income can fall (relative to the forecast rental income) before additional funds or cash reserves are needed to cover the cash shortfall. While the first breakeven ratio provides information as to the rental income level needed to show a profit, the cash breakeven ration gives the analyst an indication of the amount of rental income needed to maintain a positive cash flow.

Fixed to Total Costs. The fixed to total costs measure provides a breakdown of the project's total cost between its fixed and variable components. Real estate investments typically contain a high proportion of fixed versus variable costs, which reinforces the need to carefully evaluate a limited partnership's revenue projections. Since fixed costs do not fall as revenues decline, the investor is exposed to proportionally greater losses with declines in rental income. The higher this ratio, the greater reduction in profits is attributed to reduced revenues.

Additional Financial Indicators In addition to the above information, the system provides the user with several other tools to help in the decision-making process. Two reports also contained in the software system are the Degree of Leverage Report and the Key Ratios Report. The leverage report (Table 19.9) presents the operating, financial, and the combined leverage for the limited partnership on an annual basis for the entire hold-

Table 19.9   Leverage Report

	Degree of Leverage		
Year	Operating	Financial	Combined
1982	1.38	4.65	6.39
1983	1.49	12.26	18.21
1984	1.50	6.85	10.29
1985	1.52	4.91	7.48
1986	1.55	3.90	6.04
1987	1.90	8.39	15.97
1988	1.61	3.03	4.88
1989	1.65	2.72	4.48
1990	1.69	2.48	4.19

ing period; this allows the user to view the effects of leverage throughout the investment period.

The key ratio report (Table 19.10) presents highlights of five of the limited partnership's most important financial relationships at the start of the project's life. The first ratio, percent directly invested, reports the percentage of funds raised actually directly invested into the property. The debt to tangible asset ratio presents a measure of the amount of debt leverage involved in the venture, while the debt coverage ratio reports on the adequacy of income to service this debt. The reserve/fixed cost ratio and the days reserve available measure give the user an indication of whether the cash reserve is satisfactory.

Conclusion

The real estate analysis performed above provides the user with the financial characteristics necessary to evaluate real estate limited partnerships. Using a computer in the analysis allows the analyst to devote more time to examining the sensitivity of the investment's return to various changes in the user's assumptions.

Table 19.10   Key Ratio Report

Key Ratios

Direct investments	86.12%
Debt/tangible assets	91.45%
Debt coverage	4.5x
Reserve/fixed costs	34.39%
Days reserve available	280

Endnotes

[1] The source of this table and the other tables in the article is *Real Estate Limited Partnership Analyzer* (Haight Analytics, Ltd., 1989).

Index

About the Author

G. Timothy Haight is Professor of Finance and Chairman of the Department of Finance at Towson State University. He received his DBA in Business, Finance and Investments from George Washington University and is also President of Haight and Associates, a financial consulting firm. Dr. Haight is the author of *The New Limited Partnership Investment Advisor* (Probus 1987) and *REITS: New Opportunities In Real Estate Investment Trust Securities* (Probus 1987). He is a frequent contributor to periodicals and journals on real estate and financial topics.

Daniel Singer is Associate Professor of Finance at Towson State University. Dr. Singer is President and publisher of *Utility Investment Guide* and the author of *Investing in Utilities: A Comprehensive Industry by Industry Analysis* (Probus 1990). Dr. Singer received his PhD from the University of Colorado, his MS from the State University of New York and his BS from Rider College. He is a frequent contributor to periodicals and journals on real estate and financial topics.